ACPL, Laramie, WY   4/2019
39092100668682
Yes she can :10 stories of hope & change
Pieces:1

WITHDRAWN

P9-DWK-247

YES SHE CAN

10 STORIES OF HOPE & CHANGE FROM YOUNG FEMALE STAFFERS OF THE OBAMA WHITE HOUSE

JENNA BRAYTON, ELEANOR CELESTE, NITA CONTRERAS,
MOLLY DILLON, KALISHA DESSOURCES FIGURES,
ANDREA R. FLORES, VIVIAN P. GRAUBARD, NOEMIE C. LEVY,
TAYLOR LUSTIG & JAIMIE WOO

schwartz & wade books · new york

Albany County
Public Library
Laramie, Wyoming

A NOTE ON "SHE"

Each of the authors of this book uses the pronouns "she," "her," and "hers." We collectively chose to use the pronoun "she" for the title, yet we recognize that not all women or gender-variant people who identify with femininity use the pronoun "she," instead using other pronouns, including "they," "them," and "theirs." We celebrate gender equality and diversity. For us that means increasing the number of all kinds of women in government, especially those who are of color, those living with disabilities, and those who are LGBTQ and gender nonconforming identified, among many other identities. This book is for all of us.

Text copyright © 2019 by Jenna Brayton, Eleanor Celeste, Nita Contreras, Molly Dillon, Kalisha Dessources Figures, Andrea R. Flores, Vivian P. Graubard, Noemie C. Levy, Taylor Lustig, and Jaimie Woo

Jacket art copyright © 2019 by Samantha Hahn

All rights reserved. Published in the United States by Schwartz & Wade Books, an imprint of Random House Children's Books, a division of Penguin Random House LLC, New York.

Schwartz & Wade Books and the colophon are trademarks of Penguin Random House LLC.

Visit us on the Web! GetUnderlined.com

Educators and librarians, for a variety of teaching tools, visit us at RHTeachersLibrarians.com

Library of Congress Cataloging-in-Publication Data is available on request.
ISBN 978-1-9848-4845-1 (hc) — ISBN 978-1-9848-4846-8 (glb)
ISBN 978-1-9848-4847-5 (ebook)

The text of this book is set in 10.5-point Calluna.
Book design by Rachael Cole

Printed in the United States of America
10 9 8 7 6 5 4 3 2 1
First Edition

Random House Children's Books supports the First Amendment and celebrates the right to read.

To our mothers, grandmothers,
and all the women who came before us

This generation coming up—unselfish, altruistic, creative, patriotic—I've seen you in every corner of the country. You believe in a fair, just, inclusive America. You know that constant change has been America's hallmark, something not to fear but to embrace, and you are willing to carry this hard work of democracy forward. You'll soon outnumber any of us, and I believe as a result that the future is in good hands.

—President Barack Obama at his farewell speech in Chicago, January 10, 2017

CONTENTS

FOREWORD
BY YARA SHAHIDI

My mama has always said there's nothing more interesting than an interested human. And she's so right! It is this curiosity that human progress feeds on; but for too long, girls were not encouraged to follow their curiosity. With educational disparities and discrimination in the classroom and workplaces, the world that we occupy as women comes with the tough reality: we must persevere. Spaces only get more complicated to maneuver in when we include our various intersecting identities: ethnicity, race, sexual orientation, gender identity, religion, citizenship status, abilities, etc. But what the women who have charted maps of ingenuity, intention, and success have proved is that when women feed their potential, they in turn feed *human* potential.

We are in the midst of a cultural revolution, and women of all walks of life are leading the charge in the fight for equity! Watching this moment in history inspires me and so many of my peers to push past perceived boundaries and create new possibilities. The brilliant humans in this book represent women who *became* the change they wanted to see, feel, and experience; and in doing the work, these fierce young women have created space for others to follow suit.

I was fortunate enough to visit the Obama White House four times. In fact, President Obama once joked that I should get my own office in the White House. (I quickly closed my eyes to manifest this!) While any opportunity to be in the same room as the Obamas was a gift to me, one of the moments emblazoned on my spirit happened when I cohosted the White House Science Fair, alongside entrepreneur and educational philanthropist Karlie Kloss, under the guidance of scientist Dr. Knatokie Ford. We interviewed brilliant young scientists from around the United States about the scientific innovations and breakthroughs they were creating. Kids of all ages were turning their passions and skills into making education more accessible, creating diagnostic tests for the Ebola virus, inventing alternative power sources, and so much more! The biggest impact, however, was being surrounded by women of different generations—watching the young female scientists exhibiting their findings and Senior Advisor Valerie Jarrett and Dr. Jo Handlesman excitedly participating. The unwavering support from President Obama alongside the brilliant women of the White House, celebrating what is traditionally a male-dominated field, reinforced in me and so many others the deep and continued need for female voices in all places.

The inspiring female staffers in this book did not just "happen" to land a job in the Obama White House. They worked for it, knowing that other young women were watching and preparing to step into the spaces they created for us through their experiences—good and bad. *Yes She Can* is a gift; it's filled with ten women's inspiring stories about entering public service under the Obama Administration and how they didn't just survive but *thrived* in these spaces! These intelligent humans know the importance of their voices and values and *became* the representation that we are so lacking. Each had her own path to the White House and, once there, made her mark on the world—all while clearing a path and expanding the vision of a more inclusive America.

These women, in part, inspired me to create Eighteen x 18, an initiative to increase youth voter education and turnout. They demonstrated for me and my peers that politics can no longer happen without us—we *must* share a common love for our global community. Their stories serve as a reminder to young people that we are not alone in this fight, that there are women who have taken it upon themselves to trudge through the sometimes treacherous terrain of politics and public service in order to open the doors and let us all in. Their presence has undoubtedly carved the way for us Gen Zers, and 1 am so grateful that they have decided to share their experiences.

May our voices continue to carry the power of generations of women from the past, present, and future!

PROLOGUE

In the hallway outside the Roosevelt Room in the West Wing of the White House hang four Norman Rockwell paintings. Anyone who has worked in the White House has walked by these priceless pieces. They're part of a series—a quadriptych entitled *So You Want to See the President,* and each of the four parts features a day in the life at the center of American power. As the story goes, in late 1943, President Franklin Delano Roosevelt gave Rockwell full access to the West Wing. Rockwell spent three days sitting in the lobby, sketching all the people he saw coming and going from the front gate to the Oval Office. The paintings depict a parade of policemen, photographers, reporters, Secret Service agents, foreign diplomats, Miss America, members of Congress, White House butlers, and various West Wing staff before, in the final image, the door to the Oval Office and the President himself are revealed.

Of the fifty-eight people in these four drawings, only five are women. What's more, they show up in the White House only as

XIV ★ YES SHE CAN

secretaries, a beauty queen, and a segregated section of the U.S. military.

When President Barack Obama occupied the Oval Office, Rockwell's depiction couldn't have been more different from our reality. President Obama employed staff of all different creeds and colors. And from his first day in office, he filled a number of low- to high-level positions with women. It was 2008. Women weren't just making coffee; they were making policy. And running the show at all levels.

We were all teenagers when Barack Obama announced he was running for President. We came of age in the era of Obama, and were inspired to join the world of government by his inclusive, feminist politics. Each of us followed a unique path but had a calling that led us to the same place: the Obama White House.

Although we may have been young, the work we did might surprise you. We represented the United States government in international meetings, created public-private partnerships worth millions of dollars, led entire policy portfolios on behalf of the White House, pushed legislation on Capitol Hill, and weighed in on the President's speeches. We did it all, and more. In heels, but often in sensible flats too.

The White House was once considered an old boys' club, but the Obama White House proved that:

1. Young women get. Stuff. Done. Give us a task, vague or concrete, big or small: we'll complete it. Better than you asked for, and on or ahead of schedule.
2. Government is, as President Obama often said, made up of people. When the people are good, so is

government. And the best government reflects its
people, including women and people of color—who
make up half of *our* country.

3. Working in government is a pretty cool career choice.
   And it's something *you* can do. The prospect might be
   intimidating, but here we will show you a day in the
   life where you can see yourself too.

Most of us didn't grow up thinking that we wanted to work
in government. Even today, when you think of government, you
probably think of some dude who's been working at the same job
for forty years, on his way to a pension and retirement.

Our stories beg to differ. They show young women stepping
into the spotlight and up to the challenge, working behind the
scenes and after hours to help advance the mission of the President, his administration, and our country. These stories show
young women making big leaps and inciting change for good, but
also making mistakes and learning from them.

Since the 2016 election, women have been entering the political arena like never before. More than forty thousand of them, in
fact, according to Emily's List. These numbers are unprecedented.
But running for office is one of many ways to get involved. Every
elected official needs staffers. As you'll see, staffers help make the
policy agenda, elevate issues, and drive change. Young women are
capable, ambitious, and already changing the world, so who better to staff our government than an army of young women?

During our time at the White House, we were sleep-deprived
and overworked . . . but we would do it again in a heartbeat.
Because working in public service is worth it. *Always* worth it.

The truth is, young women have always been a part of the American story, but history hasn't always told our stories. It's time we start changing that.

As the great scholar and philosopher of our time, Beyoncé, once said . . .

Who run the world?

Girls!

—Jenna, Eleanor, Nita, Molly, Kalisha, Andrea, Vivian, Noemie, Taylor, and Jaimie
March 2019

Molly Dillon

Title: Policy Assistant for Urban Affairs, Justice and Opportunity
Office: Domestic Policy Council
Age: 25
Date: December 9, 2014

I am not a morning person. But my favorite time in the White House complex is before sunrise, when the grounds are quiet and still.

That Tuesday was one of those days when 1 arrived at work before dawn. 1 entered through the staff gate on West Executive Avenue (West Exec) and hurried up the Navy Steps into the Dwight D. Eisenhower Executive Office Building (EEOB) to drop my bag at my desk. My office was in a historic room with twenty-foot ceilings, and 1 sat with three other staffers. It's always a little weird to be one of the only souls in a building usually bustling with staff and visitors. At this point, 1 was running on about three hours of sleep but feeling wide-awake, as the adrenaline had kicked in. 1 made sure 1 had both of my phones on me—my friends always made fun of my outdated BlackBerry, but it was the official phone of White House staff, so 1 carried it like a badge of honor. 1 was barely in my office long enough to trigger the motion-sensor lights before I hurried back outside to meet a delivery truck that would be rolling up any minute.

West Exec is the small strip of parking spots separating the EEOB and the West Wing of the White House. Up until World War II, it was an actual public street. Now it's a secure avenue where the Vice President's motorcade pulls into work every day. It's also where members of the President's Cabinet enter the White House, and occasionally where the President of the United States (POTUS) crosses to attend meetings inside the EEOB. But that morning, as the December fog rolled in, it was just me, a young policy staffer, waiting for a delivery truck filled with movie-screening equipment.

I checked my BlackBerry—6:45 a.m. The sun wouldn't be up for another half hour or so, but morning was starting to break. I scrolled through my emails; double-, triple-, quadruple-checking the tick-tock—that's White House lingo for the minute-to-minute schedule breakdown of a White House event. I'd spent part of the past weekend at my desk writing up personalized schedules for every staffer and intern helping out that day, so everyone knew where they needed to be and when. It's the best way to prevent something from going wrong—and of course, something *will* go wrong—but I figured I might as well try to anticipate, and possibly prevent, multiple scenarios. I committed the most important times to memory:

7:00 a.m.—Truck arrives
8:00 a.m.—Film preview
2:00 p.m.—Youth meeting
4:00 p.m.—Guests arrive
5:00 p.m.—Showtime

I glanced at the West Wing to my left and thought about the dozen or so staffers who sat behind a row of fake windows adorned with flower boxes. From the outside, you'd never know that was the Situation Room, and that even at this hour—at all hours, in fact—it was buzzing with activity. Members of the President's National Security staff were inside assessing global threats, evaluating intelligence, and preparing presidential briefings. Even though I spent almost five years in the White House, I'm still impressed by the sheer amount of work that got done by so few people. It's something I wish more people knew.

I looked over to the EEOB on my right. It's my favorite building in DC. Completed in 1888, it once housed the State Department, the Department of the Navy, and the War Department. They've all since moved out, or reorganized, as they outgrew the space. Now it's where the majority of the President's staff sits, including me. And in just a few hours, the EEOB will be host to a series of policy announcements—brand-new rules and programs from more than ten different federal agencies, states, and nonprofit organizations to make the lives of children in foster care better. We'd also be welcoming more than one hundred young people in foster care and a bunch of VIP guests, including mega movie stars and the Vice President of the United States.

And the reason I'm the one standing there so early? I'm the one who organized it all.

★ ★ ★

Let me back up. What does someone working in policy even do?

Most people see the words *policy* and *White House* and think of the strategies and courses of action a government takes—like executive orders and laws. But in reality, policy is so much more. It's a number of things—including (*especially* including) how the White House chooses to spend its most limited resource: time. The issues we highlighted, the events we organized, even who we invited to the table to be part of the discussion. When the White House does *anything,* it means something. It brings an automatically heightened level of attention and legitimacy to an issue, organization, or person.

Oftentimes, policy also means change, and when you're fighting the status quo, change can be really hard. In thinking about progress, and especially civil rights, Megan Smith, President Obama's Chief Technology Officer, liked to remind us of a quote from our third president, Thomas Jefferson:

> Laws and institutions must go hand in hand with the progress of the human mind. As that becomes more developed, more enlightened, as new discoveries are made, new truths discovered and manners and opinions change with the change of circumstances, institutions must advance also to keep pace with the times.

Jefferson is a controversial figure, but he has a point here: even if certain advances make some people uncomfortable, this is a country built on change. We're always evolving. I don't think the founding fathers could have anticipated what 2014 would look like. They would certainly be surprised by the number of women working at the White House, not to mention our African American president. As President Obama said:

America's greatness is a testament to generations of courageous individuals who, in the face of uncomfortable truths, accepted that the work of perfecting our nation is unending and strived to expand the reach of freedom to all.

Our work to expand that reach of freedom to all, no matter what you look like, where you come from, the color of your skin, how you worship, or who you love, was our ongoing effort to form a more perfect union.

Working for President Obama, I learned that as important and far-reaching an institution as the White House is, it was easy to become isolated from real people living and dealing with the issues we were trying to address. For much of America, DC is far away, both figuratively and literally. To make sure that he was hearing from people outside our bubble, the President asked our Correspondence Office to give him ten letters a day. He wanted them to reflect the overall pool of letters coming in, so some were happy with his performance, and others . . . not so happy. I signed up for a special internal email list that allowed me to read those ten letters too. It was a good way to take the pulse of the nation. And while we met with advocacy groups nearly every day, that's not *quite* the same as doing on-the-ground work. So that's why, across every White House office, it was not uncommon to find staff going out of their way to connect with our constituents—the entire country—in unique ways to make sure they knew we were listening.

A good number of those letters came from young people. They shared their hopes and dreams, their fears and challenges.

In President Obama, they found a champion. And in them, the President found a duty. The creation of the My Brother's Keeper initiative to improve the lives of boys and young men of color is one example of many policies created by President Obama. Making sure that no young person's circumstance of birth determines their destiny was a headlining mission and the writing on the wall—literally! The walls of the West Wing, and almost every office, were filled with jumbos—blown-up versions of photos taken by the President's photographers. Many were candid shots of the President with kids. (#Obamaandkids later became its own glorious hashtag.) So it's not at all surprising that he made it a priority to help some of the most underserved children in America—children who don't have the love and support every child deserves—and many of these children are in foster care. We would use whatever tools we had to carry out the President's goal.

To put it very simply, working in this White House meant creating and identifying positive change, connecting to the people you were helping, and then making sure the word got out. It was a lot more than that too, but these things were a huge part of my job.

Where does this change come from? Well, as it turns out, sometimes from a junior staffer like me.

★ ★ ★

In early 2014, my teammate Sonali Patel was nearing the end of her temporary stint in the White House, after which she would be returning to the Department of Health and Human Services. Sonali was the point person on all things child welfare, and when she left, someone else would have to lead that work. The head of our team, my boss, Roy L. Austin Jr., told me he wanted me to take over Sonali's child welfare portfolio and help make foster care a bigger, even more prominent issue in the White House. "Owning" a policy portfolio means that you are the staffer who is responsible for moving an issue forward, answering any questions from senior staff, and alerting them to problems before they become crises.

My initial reaction was to be excited—my boss was trusting me with a huge policy portfolio, and I hadn't even turned twenty-five yet! While I had been working on policy since I'd arrived, this was the first portfolio that was all mine. *Omg I have a policy portfolio at the freaking White House!*

And then it hit me—*OMG, I HAVE A POLICY PORTFOLIO AT THE FREAKING WHITE HOUSE.* [Cue panic.]

Its success or failure depended on me. And while there were ultimate-decision makers above me and I knew about child welfare, I remember thinking, *There's no way I know enough about this to be the lead.* Turns out that the little unqualified voice telling you you're a fraud actually has a name: imposter syndrome. It's an uninvited guest that will try to derail you.

There's so much more to learn.

You'll never be able to grasp it all.

You're inevitably going to ask a stupid question in a meeting and they're all gonna figure out you don't know what you're talking about. You'll never be given any responsibilities again. They'll make you turn in your badge and Secret Service will escort you out the gate.

Maybe I should have just said "no, thanks!"

But then I thought, Roy is smart. He's a former federal prosecutor. He helped lead the Department of Justice Civil Rights Division, and was now a Deputy Assistant to the President—not to mention one of the most senior African American men in the White House. If Roy trusted me to handle this, maybe he saw something in me that I didn't see in myself. I had been working for Roy for only about two months, but I really liked him and didn't want to let him down (not to mention the President!). I wanted him to think I was smart and compassionate and capable.

So I gave myself a pep talk.

This is what you went to college for.

This is why you went to grad school for public policy.

This is why you applied for a White House internship, even though you knew no one in the building and the odds of getting chosen were tiny. And, when you got that internship, why you worked your butt off every day, often the first one at your desk in the morning and the last to leave at night.

This opportunity was also why I had spent the past six months as a sponge, absorbing as much as possible and trying *really* hard not to mess up. It was my first real job, and I didn't want people to think someone had made a mistake in hiring me. When I wrote a memo or talking points and staff more senior than me made changes, I read all their edits and saw how they made my words better. I watched their style, their work ethic, their routines. I absorbed it all. In such a busy workplace, most people didn't have time to sit down and explain why they made the changes they did. I did my best to learn from experience. Their edits were my feedback.

I doubled down and read as much as I could about foster care and started meeting with as many experts as possible. The more I learned about this massive institution, the more I learned about the cracks in the system and the different types of kids affected. There are over 400,000 young people in foster care, 74 percent of whom are there due to neglect issues—mainly due to poverty. Each year, over 20,000 youth in care age out, meaning that they become eighteen-year-old independent adults having not been adopted. Becoming an adult is hard enough. Imagine doing it with few resources and little to no support. Compared to their peers, a disproportionate number of young people who have been in foster care are in the juvenile or criminal justice systems, abusing drugs, experiencing homelessness, and/or facing significant mental health crises. And a disproportionate number of the young people who have been in care are kids of color. This isn't a small problem, and it isn't going to be solved by one big policy change. I was, truthfully, overwhelmed. But I had to try to do something to improve their lives.

After I took over the portfolio, Roy and I decided that to really bring awareness to the issue of foster care and impel action on the subject nationwide, we needed to create some sort of announcement, something extra special that had never been done before.

While sitting at the stately wooden conference table in his office a few weeks after Sonali left, Roy asked me if I had seen the trailer for the new *Annie* movie. In this updated version, Annie was in foster care. The cast had been announced and included major stars like Jamie Foxx and Cameron Diaz. He suggested we do a screening of the film to launch our next round of policy announcements—and fill the room with kids in foster care.

We had never done an event that large on this issue, but it wasn't unusual for the White House to host screenings of movies before they went to theaters—especially if they had a message related to our work. Plus, in the original movie, Annie goes to the White House to sing for President FDR! Perfect! After a quick Google search (I think most people would be shocked at the amount of policy work that starts with just googling things) to see which studio was putting the movie out (Sony), Roy contacted a friend from law school who just happened to work there. Roy's friend introduced us to Keith Weaver, Sony's Vice President for Worldwide Government Affairs. Keith was excited about this potential collaboration. We went back and forth with him on details and worked with the White House Counsel's Office (our team of lawyers) to make sure we followed all the rules and laws, and within a few weeks, Sony agreed! They would bring *Annie* and its cast to the White House, and we would build an event around it. I had my next long-term assignment, and it was time to get to work.

I spent the next few months working on my everyday responsibilities, including the unexpected fire drills (i.e., "Drop everything and do this!"), while creating, planning, and executing a major White House event and announcement and trying to become an expert in foster care.

One of the most important things I learned from this job was how to ask smart questions—and that asking questions doesn't mean you're dumb. In fact, it often means quite the opposite. I listened to Roy ask questions in meetings, and it's a skill I sharpened just by observing him.

A lucky thing about working in the Obama White House was that everyone was not just smart but also kind. Coworkers like Rafael López (an education policy advisor), Sherry Lachman (one of the Vice President's policy advisors), and JooYeun Chang (the head of the Children's Bureau at the Department of Health and Human Services) all sat down with me more than once and answered approximately one million questions. They were always willing to listen, explain, and work through problems. That's the Obama Administration for you. That's also the reason I sought out the help of my colleague Jodi Gillette, the President's Senior Policy Advisor for Native American Affairs.

One of the most disproportionately impacted groups in the foster care system is the Native American community. There is a long and shameful history of the U.S. government neglecting, or actively hurting, the indigenous peoples of this country, including taking Native kids from their homes and shipping them to schools that stripped them of their family traditions and sometimes even their names. This cruelty has spawned poverty, as well as drug and alcohol abuse, which has caused many Native American children to be removed from their families and placed in foster homes, often far away from their tribes.

Jodi told me stories of young people torn from their communities, their culture, and their traditions. The Indian Child Welfare Act (ICWA) of 1978 was meant to address the complicated relationship between tribes and state child welfare systems by prioritizing placements with family members for children in foster care so they could stay closer to their reservation, kin, and identity. ICWA helped, but not nearly as much as it should have.

Armed with new research, I reconvened a team of agency staffers across the federal government that Sonali had organized when she was leading the portfolio. Since many agencies were doing work that affected kids in foster care, it was up to the White House to make sure agencies were working together toward the goals of the Administration. I once heard a young man who had been in foster care say "'Foster kid' is a legal status, not a personality trait." We, as an administration, needed to make sure more people understood that.

At the White House, we often announced new policy through some sort of event. Doing so helped to encourage a broad set of agencies to come up with new ideas and shine a spotlight on complex issues. The goal for my event was to tell Americans, especially young people in foster care, that their needs were a priority to the White House. So when it came time to figure out who the guests at our event should be, it was immediately clear who belonged in the audience: kids in foster care. Make no mistake, it would definitely have been easier to just invite a bunch of adults working for advocacy groups and kids in foster care from around the DC area. But I wasn't going for easy. That's not the example the President was setting, and it wasn't what I would settle for. I knew the work wasn't done right if it wasn't inclusive. If this was truly the People's House, this event wouldn't be complete without kids who represented the *entire* country.

But how to do that when you are working with a budget of zero dollars?

Because the details weren't public yet, I couldn't say too much to anyone invited from the outside. So I contacted different foster care organizations across the country, extending invites to a vague event, giving them each a handful of slots, and advising them to use them primarily for young people who were currently in foster care. Some of these organizations had never been invited to the White House before and were thrilled to use their own funds to fly or bus kids to Washington for the opportunity. The groups shared with us what a difference it could make in the lives of young people who had already experienced so much trauma. It would have been ten times harder for me to find young people on my own, so we reached out to those who were already connected. This method is central to organizing—you don't always have to reinvent the wheel. Odds are, there are amazing groups doing the work that you're trying to plug into. Welcome them, ask what you can do to help, and bring together everyone working toward the same goals.

And so our guest list started to grow. And grow. And grow.

On any given day, there are many White House events, so naturally, they can't all be attended by the President or Vice President. But Sherry Lachman said she'd ask if the Vice President would be able to stop by. Sherry was actually in foster care for a period of time when she was a kid and then went on to earn three Ivy League degrees, work in the United States Senate and the White House, and, a few years after this event, start her own foster care organization, Foster America. (Obama people are the *most* impressive.) Sherry had her own (more than) full-time job, but she still found time to pitch in to make this event extra special. I tried not to get my hopes up, because the VP's schedule was always exceedingly busy. It turned out, though, that Vice President Biden's daughter Ashley runs a nonprofit organization in Delaware that works with children in foster care, and Sherry had the brilliant idea to pitch this as something they could do together. About two weeks before the big day, we got word: the Biden father-daughter duo was going to attend! This was *huge.* Their participation would shine a brighter spotlight on the work we'd been doing and would make a big difference in our goal of gaining more visibility for the issue of foster care.

★★★

With the Vice President set to attend, it felt like all the pieces were coming together. And after months of research and preparation, I found myself on West Exec just as the sun was rising. A white truck appeared at the southwest appointment gate. I waved it over and helped the Sony team bring their equipment into our auditorium. As part of my (approximately) one-million-point prep plan, I had to ask the team that ran the auditorium to arrive early to supervise setup. These guys were all career staff (they stay in their jobs no matter who the President is) and were some of the hardest-working, nicest people in the building. Whatever event you wanted to hold in their space, they helped to make it happen.

First things first: that morning, I needed to make sure the movie actually played. Sony agreed to let us screen the film, provided we use their special DVD player, which produced a higher-quality picture than ours. There was a chance it wouldn't connect to our system, and I had been losing sleep over this prospect for weeks. What was a movie premiere without a movie? (We asked them to bring a backup, regular DVD just in case. But what if that one didn't work either?) I grabbed a seat in the front row for the test run, and at first, nothing appeared on the screen. *Please, please, please let it work,* I pleaded to myself. Suddenly, the Sony Pictures logo appeared and music burst through the speakers. HALLELUJAH. Now I could move on to worrying about the rest of the day.

Shortly after we successfully connected, Roy walked into the room. Even though we thought we had checked every box, the day before the event, the Vice President's staff asked us if we had watched the movie yet. Roy and I looked at each other. Neither of us had watched it—we didn't think we needed to. . . . It was *Annie*! Everyone knows *Annie.* It's rated PG. What could possibly

be a problem? We were informed that someone from the White House needed to watch the film to make sure that there was nothing inappropriate or the VP could not participate. Yikes.

So Roy came in extra early to watch *Annie* with me before work. (If someone at his level approved of the content, we would be able to say it was cleared.) You truly haven't lived until you've watched an entire movie at eight a.m., at work. (This is not something I could have predicted spending my time on when I accepted the position the year before.)

When we were finally done screening the film and the crew had left campus until later in the afternoon, I headed back to my desk. Waiting for me was a muffin, a fruit cup, and a Post-it note that read "Congrats! Today will be great! Don't forget to eat. . . ." It was from Becky Monroe, a civil rights attorney and one of my teammates. I could have cried at her thoughtfulness, and at the sight of food. (I hadn't eaten anything yet that morning!)

But that day was not just about the movie screening and the celebrities. It was also, and primarily, about the young people.

Starting in early 2014, Secretary of Education Arne Duncan had been hosting listening sessions with students. Called "Student Voices," the meetings were held to regularly engage in discussions with young people, using their perspectives to help increase connections between the Education Department's work and the needs of students. In addition to all the other challenges they face, young people in foster care are at abnormally high risk of dropping out of high school and are unlikely to attend, let alone graduate from, college. In a chaotic life, school is often one of the only stable things they have to hang on to, but the education system doesn't always address their unique needs.

There's a saying in the civil rights world: *Nothing about us, without us.* Who knows these issues better than the people living them? So before our main event, and with Jodi's help, I organized a Student Voices sit-down with Secretary Duncan, Secretary of the Interior Sally Jewell, and fifteen Native American youths in foster care.

Right before the meeting started, I made a last-minute decision to remove all the adults from the room, myself included, except for the two Secretaries and one tribal liaison. I looked around the crowded room at all the chaperones and federal government staffers. I wanted the young people to be able to open up. They should feel like the White House was a safe space where they could speak honestly about their lives. They shouldn't feel like fish in a bowl, with a bunch of grown-up eyes on them, no matter how well-meaning we all were. I was later told that the meeting, slated for two hours, lasted nearly three, and by the end, there wasn't a dry eye in the room.

With all the talk you see on the news of political wins and losses and personalities, it too easily gets lost that people in government are just that—*people.* Even Secretaries. Everyone was there because they wanted to help. That's why President Obama appointed us. At every level of this government, we wanted to make lives better. We all wanted equality *and* equity.

★ ★ ★

This unexpected schedule change gave me some extra time to get work done. I headed back to my desk and answered a bunch of emails (I still had my regular job to do). And then with my ace team of interns, all of us with our personalized tick-tock in hand, we started setting up the auditorium. We arranged nearly two hundred name tags, each printed under the White House logo on fancy card stock, in alphabetical order on a welcome table. I didn't *need* to make name tags for everyone, but I knew that our guests, many of whom had traveled from far away, might like a small keepsake. (It was an extra hour or two of work over the weekend, but I wanted them to have something they could physically hold on to, to remember the day. Again . . . budget of $0.00.)

We put the fact sheets on the same table. Policy fact sheets provide background info on a topic and short descriptions of policy changes, and are often sent to the media or used at press conferences or events like ours. We had been working for about six months on this fact sheet, which was nearly four pages long and included a number of new policy announcements.

Nothing in the White House happens with just one person, but I was the one ultimately responsible for pushing the agencies to make their announcements ready and then compiling and screening everything before it went to senior officials and before it went to print.

I was especially proud of our announcement from the Departments of Education and Agriculture: a letter about free school meals. To the outside world, a letter might not sound like a big deal, but this one was *so* important, and was an issue requested by the foster care community. Back in 2010, President Obama had signed the Healthy, Hunger-Free Kids Act. Part of that law said that anyone in foster care was eligible for free school lunch and wouldn't need to apply for the program. But in practice, schools sometimes didn't know which kids were in foster care, and then the eligible students went hungry because they didn't have money for lunch and they weren't marked for a free meal. The organizations responsible weren't communicating. The two departments, together with help from the White House, sent a "Dear Colleague" letter to every school in the country, outlining what the law does and the best ways to make sure no young person in foster care went hungry at school. I had read extensively about this issue and met with experts, and ultimately worked with the departments to write and send out that letter. It was going to make a big difference.

Altogether, we were announcing twelve new items, including actions around financial protection and literacy, improving maternal health care, increasing access to jobs, improving education, eradicating homelessness, and redoubling efforts to make sure the Indian Child Welfare Act was followed.

With the handouts and name tags in place, I looked over the guest list one more time. There were nearly two hundred individuals attending, including some pretty high-profile people, like Secretary of Agriculture Tom Vilsack, the former governor of Iowa, who had himself lived in an orphanage as a young child. He was happy to participate, tell his story, and share the good work his department was doing. Then there was Director Will Gluck and actors Jamie Foxx, Cameron Diaz, Rose Byrne, Bobby Cannavale, and eleven-year-old Quvenzhané Wallis—all the stars of the film had agreed to attend. We even got Jamie, Cameron, and Quvenzhané to film a PSA on adoption and foster care. I wrote the script, they filmed it during their press tour, and we would show it at our event and post it online. Hearing them speak the words I wrote for the video was a wild feeling.

But I was most excited about meeting the young people. I really wanted the event to mean something to them.

Before I knew it, the auditorium started to fill. My meticulous spreadsheets transformed into actual people who would be affected by the policies announced that night. I could feel my heart swell. I took a moment to look around. Many of our guests were high school students, right around the age I was when President Obama announced he was running for office.

And now, almost eight years after that Springfield speech, here I was, working for the White House, in this auditorium, at an event that I planned from scratch, where there were definitely more people than seats, as guests and staff had begun to line the side and back walls. Someone brought in more folding chairs from elsewhere in the building. We were at max capacity.

I had been preparing for this day for months, trying to imagine everything that could go wrong and making contingency plans to prevent disaster. But even with the best-laid plans, something is *always* going to go wrong. Tonight was no exception.

You can imagine that obtaining security clearance for two hundred people to enter the White House can be a logistical nightmare. Everyone has to submit something called a WAVE form to be cleared ahead of time by the Secret Service. WAVEs contain personal information like your name and birthday and social security number, and are submitted for a specific date and time. And here's the most important detail: guests have exactly one hour before and one hour after that specific time during which they can enter the building.

I arrived at the West Wing gate a few minutes before four o'clock to escort the Sony group in. I'd had the opportunity to meet a few famous people (Hollywood famous and DC famous) since working at the White House, but it's always sort of a shock to the brain when you meet someone you've only ever seen on TV or in the movies. That was how I felt seeing Cameron Diaz—she was tall and stylish and, as it turns out, extremely nice. While I silently fought the urge to tell her how many times I watched *Charlie's Angels* in middle school, a Sony executive very calmly and kindly informed me that Jamie Foxx's flight was delayed. He wouldn't land at Reagan National Airport for at least another forty-five minutes. I looked at my tick-tock and tried *very hard* not to panic. The event was planned down to the minute. I didn't want to make our young guests wait, but we couldn't start without Jamie. Plus, he had a seat front row, center. We explained to the Vice President's staff that Jamie's plane was delayed, and they were incredibly flexible and understanding.

Finally, after what felt like an eternity but was probably closer to an hour, I got word that Jamie's plane had landed and he was on his way. I exited the complex to greet him and escort his group directly to the event. Even celebrities have to show their ID to Secret Service—and that was when the agents at the gate informed me . . . he wasn't cleared to enter the building. His WAVEs had expired! He had flown all the way to DC, and now he wasn't allowed to enter the event. This was my fault; I should have remembered that he would need to be recleared.

Before I even had a chance to be furious with myself for not anticipating that this would happen, I sent out a mass email to other junior staffers to see if anyone was at their computer and could resubmit his information. My friend Taylor Lustig came to the rescue by rushing to her desk and sending Jamie's WAVEs in for the current time. And after a very cold thirty-seven-degree

(December in DC!) ten-minute wait outside at the gate, we were finally in. At this point, I had apologized profusely, and I will say that Jamie was very cool about it.

After months of painstaking work, I was upset, and it was a hard feeling to shake. Recognizing that we still had the entire night ahead of us, I basically had to quickly but sternly lecture myself: *Do not let this snafu get in the way of the event or your ability to enjoy it. You fixed it. You can't change the past, only how you carry yourself moving forward. Also, let's make sure never to make this mistake again.*

I emailed the Vice President's staff from my BlackBerry to tell them that we were all here and whenever he was ready, we would begin.

The Sony group and I waited in a small greenroom. After a few minutes, the door opened and in walked Vice President Biden with his daughter Ashley. I had had the privilege of watching him speak in person before and had seen him around the White House, but it was still totally surreal whenever he entered the room. Even the stars were starstruck. He walked right up to Cameron and gave her a big hug; same with Jamie. The Vice President's photographer snapped a few photos of him with the cast, flanked by American flags, before we headed to our places.

The Vice President was kicking off the speaking program, so our *Annie* crew filed into the auditorium to take their reserved front-row seats. The second they stepped through the doors, the room exploded in applause. Many of the young people physically jumped up from their chairs, phones at the ready to snap a picture of a real-life movie star. The energy was palpable. The Vice President, meanwhile, had ventured farther backstage to a secure room used whenever he or the President spoke in this auditorium. A Secret Service agent appeared and stood outside the room's door, staring straight ahead.

I smoothed out my lucky black J. Crew dress and rolled down the sleeves of my light pink Topshop blazer (an outfit I had planned weeks in advance) and asked Secret Service to let me through. I would be introducing the Vice President onstage. This was Roy's idea. I would never have put myself in that role, but he told me I had done all the work and I'd earned it. I closed the binder I had put together for the event, tucked it under my arm, and took a deep breath before walking through the door to greet the Vice President.

In that tiny cordoned-off area, it was just me, Vice President Biden, and his daughter Ashley. To be honest, I don't remember exactly what I said to him—I kind of blacked out for a moment because I was so nervous. I *think* I said something along the lines of "Thank you so much for being here and speaking to the group." And he thanked me for including him; he was glad to be there. All three of us were excited to begin.

I walked out onto the stage and the room quieted down. The lights were brighter than I expected and I blinked, trying to focus on the paper in front of me. I made a mental note to thank my parents for suggesting I join my high school's debate team. All those years of debate might not have made me the "coolest," but at least I was no stranger to speaking in front of a crowd. Although this was a REALLY big crowd . . . which didn't even include the thousands of people watching live on WhiteHouse.gov. I'd had the good sense to type up my short introduction, so I had a script to follow. I introduced myself and got to be the first person to officially welcome our audience to the White House. I thanked my boss, Roy; my colleagues; and the group from Sony. I paused for a beat; then I said, "Please welcome the Vice President of the United States, Joe Biden, and his daughter, Ashley Biden, Executive Director of the Delaware Center for Justice."

The Vice President and Ashley entered to grand applause, both with big, warm smiles on their faces. We shook hands, and I stepped off the stage (without tripping, falling, or anything else disastrous). I exhaled for maybe the first time all day.

Ashley spoke first, about the incredible work she's doing at her organization in Delaware, the importance of smart foster care policy, and investing in our nation's young people. The Vice President was standing at her side *beaming.* You could tell how proud he is of her. As she concluded, she introduced her dad.

So there's a not-so-well-kept secret about the Vice President around the White House. You may schedule him for, let's say, ten minutes of remarks. You may brief him that he has ten minutes for remarks. He may only have ten minutes' worth of remarks written by his speechwriters. But it is almost guaranteed that if Vice President Biden is speaking at your event . . . he's going to speak longer than planned. That's just who he is. He's passionate about his work, especially when it comes to kids. That evening, when he was scheduled for ten minutes, he stayed onstage for twenty, giving what I think (although I may be biased) was one of the best speeches I've ever heard him give.

Speaking solemnly of the tragic accident that took the lives of his wife and young daughter, he told the room:

> I know from personal experience, as most people in here know, that life can change in an instant. All of it can change. And when life throws challenges your way and when things happen that are unfair, or even

unspeakable, things that no kids should have to deal with alone, it's hard to stay focused on achieving your goals and even having dreams sometimes. It's hard to believe in yourself. It's hard to believe in yourself when it feels nobody out there cares. But you look around this room. There's a lot of adults in here [who] care a lot. And Ashley cares. The President cares.

The weight of the moment was not lost on us. I scanned the faces of my coworkers in the room, and I knew we were all thinking the same thing: This work mattered. It mattered that this group was here. It mattered that the Biden family was here. It mattered because the Vice President of the United States was telling kids in foster care that *they* mattered, and that the President had their back.

He ended with a challenge to all the young people in the room: "I'm counting on you to help those kids who might not be as strong or resilient as you. Kids who, if you remember, are scared right now. Your example, you've got to point out to them, you've got to show them, that there is a rainbow for them."

We were running far behind schedule, but no one cared because no one wanted him to wrap. And when he did, the entire room rose from their seats for an extended ovation.

I thought, *The evening can't possibly get better than the Vice President's speech.*

I was wrong.

The youngest speaker of the night was John, a sixteen-year-old high school student in foster care. For every grown-up speaking, I wanted one young person speaking too. My education policy colleague Rafael and I had reached out to Communities in Schools, an organization bringing kids to the event, to see if they had anyone who they thought would be up to the challenge. They immediately said, "John." John was introducing Secretary Vilsack, but first he was going to introduce himself. He stepped up to the podium and took a shaky breath. When he began to speak, you could just tell—he was *so* nervous. Which was fair! Speaking in front of a large crowd at any age, let alone at sixteen, is nerve-racking.

He began with his name and age and how long he had been in foster care. He was looking down at his notes, not making eye contact with the audience. His shoulders were hunched, his hands hidden in his pockets.

Powering through and hardly looking up, he spoke quietly into the microphone. Then he told the room that before becoming involved with Communities in Schools, he used to skip class and got bad grades. But he was changing that. Now his grades were better. He had perfect attendance. And one day, he was going to college.

Suddenly, we heard a burst of solo applause. Jamie Foxx had leapt out of his chair in the front row, directly in front of John and the podium, clapping loudly. John looked up for the first time, totally confused, and their eyes locked. For a moment, the only people standing in the room were John and Jamie. Then the entire room was applauding, rising from their chairs.

It was like watching a person thaw. John's shoulders relaxed, he stood up taller, and a huge smile spread across his face, like a light was radiating from within him that had just been flipped on.

John had spent a good portion of his life without supportive adults, and now here he was at the White House, sharing an intimate wish about his hopes and dreams with a room full of people.

At that moment, I knew that when I'm old and gray and telling my grandchildren about what it was like to work in the Obama White House, I'll tell them about the look in John's eyes when he realized one of the biggest movie stars in the world was standing and clapping for him. Not too long before, John had given up on himself. Now here he was, advocating for himself, telling himself and the world that he mattered. And the world told him back, "Yes. You do."

The rest of the night was a blur of speakers and panels, including all the major stars onstage together, moderated by Roy. I got to just stand back and enjoy it all (and make sure the program followed the right order).

When all the speakers had finished and the lights finally dimmed, the Sony Pictures logo appeared on-screen and music played through the speakers. I thought of the White House's nickname: the People's House. That night, I felt we'd lived up to that ideal.

As the movie played, as the kids laughed and cheered at a story with a main character who was just like them, I reflected on what we had pulled off that day. The demands on everyone at the White House are a lot. The stakes are high all the time. We were only temporary executors of that building, and the odds that any of us would be there at all, POTUS included, were so small. This formula gives you crazy perspective. That eight-year clock is ticking, and ticking loudly. I worked thirteen-, fourteen-, fifteen-hour days, and every night, I still walked out the front gates thinking I need to do more. (If only I didn't have to sleep or eat!) For a few minutes, though, that voice disappeared and I absorbed the magic of the evening.

What we did at the White House affected people's lives in

ways we'll never see or be able to quantify. But that night, as I watched a room full of joyful young people from my seat in the back, my colleagues—my teammates—sitting around me, I knew we had done something objectively, tangibly good. It was a nice feeling. I mentally filed it away, like a reserve stash of hope for the tough days inevitably to come. Nights like this are what help get you through.

ANDREA R. FLORES

Title: Policy Assistant for Immigration and Rural Affairs
Office: Domestic Policy Council
Age: 25
Date: June 27, 2013

I never thought I could work in politics, much less the White House.

I grew up the youngest of three children in a Mexican American household; no one in my family was politically involved. When I wasn't practicing the viola, I was reading every newspaper and magazine article I could find about what was happening in Washington, DC.

The idea that I could have a career in politics seemed unrealistic because there were so few women of color in the stories I was reading—sometimes you need to see yourself in a place to believe you belong there.

It wasn't until college that I gave politicking a try. In 2006, as a freshman at Harvard, I ran for the Undergraduate Council (UC), our student government. After knocking on *every single door* in my quarter of Harvard yard, I won my very first election. I was surprised and ecstatic—I couldn't believe I had convinced enough people to vote for me!

When I won, the college newspaper asked if I had run on a Latinx agenda (I was one of six women on the thirty-two-person council and the only Latinx member). I said no—I ran on a student agenda. I didn't want to be seen as different from the other newly elected freshman representatives, and I thought it was strange that a college reporter was asking me about my identity in a student government election.

Like most extracurricular organizations at Harvard, the UC took itself very seriously. We were a microcosm of politics at the state and national levels: mostly white, mostly male, and unwelcoming to anyone who broke that mold. It was clear from my first day on the council that I was different. I was small, brown, incredibly idealistic, and unsure of myself. But as I got to know the other council members, I began to sense that I could do this. For the next three and a half years, I gave everything I had to the UC.

As one of the few women on the council, I was a controversial figure. I often experienced male classmates telling me how I should or should not act on student government—even if they weren't on the council themselves. Many of them told me that I didn't seem like the "type" of person who could succeed on the UC. One called me on the phone over the summer to tell me I was bad at politics and should go back to playing the viola. One told me I wasn't outgoing enough for campus politics, much less real politics. Three times, I made men on the UC so mad that they yelled in my face. One pushed a table into me at a coffee shop in Harvard Square. As a Latina, serving on the UC was never easy. Sometimes it was incredibly painful.

Being Mexican American hasn't always been a comfortable

identity for me. As far back as I can remember, my parents used to tell me that I would face challenges because our country hadn't accepted the Latinx community as truly American. That while I might enjoy the full benefits of citizenship, there would always be people who questioned my presence in certain places.

These lessons didn't make sense in New Mexico, where the population and community leaders were predominantly Latinx. But in college, where my classmates were predominantly white, my parents' words began to sink in and shape the person I became. On my first day of college, for instance, a classmate (who also ended up on the UC) told me that in order to fix our immigration system, the government should just shoot a few immigrants as they crossed the border, to send a message. I didn't know how to respond.

Over time, I started to believe the people who said I couldn't hack it on the UC. Even in the low-stakes environment of college student government, I internalized the message that I didn't belong.

But on November 4, 2008, I witnessed a political event that made me feel bolder. I remember watching the presidential election results with classmates and crying off and on as I processed that the country had elected a member of a racial minority to the highest office in the land. Just when I had begun to believe that I didn't belong on the UC, President Obama's election made me determined to prove that I did.

In the following weeks, I decided it was my turn to step up. Time to face my fear and discomfort and run for Harvard's most prominent elected position: student body president. I wanted to change the tone of campus politics by making the UC, and the college, more inclusive for all Harvard students.

The two-week campaign was . . . terrible. People made fun of my heavy black eyeliner and said I didn't seem genuine. A campus blog superimposed my face onto New Mexico governor Bill Richardson's body. But the worst part of the election was the way the college newspaper covered it. Articles written about me never failed to mention two things: one, that I am Latina, and two, that I was not the "typical" candidate. The irony of this framing was that I was absolutely the typical candidate. I had served five straight semesters on the UC, led the finance committee, and balanced our budget with a surplus. But none of these achievements mattered because of who I was: a woman of color trying to be elected to the most visible position on campus. It didn't help that I was also running against a popular member of Harvard's exclusive final clubs.

When I won, I surprised everyone, including myself. I was the first Latinx student body president of Harvard. It was my job to represent the interests of the entire campus to college administrators and to run the UC. The college newspaper observed that I seemed surprised and anxious when I heard the news—and this time they were right. Even though I was proud of the outcome, I was afraid to embrace my new role.

This discomfort with myself, as a Latina leading the UC, became apparent to others. My first semester leading the council ended with a newspaper article questioning whether I had the personality to be a leader. It wasn't until President Obama nominated Sonia Sotomayor to the Supreme Court, in the spring of 2009, that I knew what was holding me back: as I watched her confirmation hearings in tears, I realized she had made peace with the fact that her identity was always going to be a topic of interest. As she used her skills as a lawyer to defend herself from senators criticizing her speech about being a "wise Latina,"

I began to think that maybe whitewashing my identity wasn't my best path forward.

When I worked at the White House for President Obama's immigration team, I began to understand how to become the Latinx leader I wanted to be.

★ ★ ★

When I graduated from college in 2010, I applied for a job in President Obama's Administration, hoping to work on his immigration policy. In 2008, he'd promised to bring forward comprehensive immigration reform legislation, and I wanted to be part of changing the system.

It was a long shot, because thousands of other college graduates were doing the same, but in July 2011, I received a call from the President's Personnel Office—they wanted me to interview for a political appointment at the Department of Homeland Security (DHS). After a successful interview, I became a presidential appointee at United States Citizenship and Immigration Services (USCIS), the government agency that operates our country's immigration system.

While working on a project at USCIS in the fall of 2012, I met Felicia Escobar, the head of the White House immigration team. I didn't know it at the time, but Felicia was looking for a junior immigration staffer to help her, Esther Olavarria, and Tyler Moran make President Obama's goal of passing immigration reform a reality.

When President Obama was reelected in 2012, those of us in the immigration field knew that immigration reform would be his next big priority. By the end of that year, it seemed as though all of Washington agreed that the time was right for Congress to act. In January 2013, a group of eight senators (all men—four Republicans, four Democrats) came together and put forward a bill. They called themselves the Gang of Eight, and their staff began working with the White House immigration team to create what would soon be known as S.744.

After I met her for coffee in January 2013, Felicia told me that she was impressed with my work at USCIS and asked me to defer law school to work at the White House for the next year. I said yes with little hesitation. Even though I had planned to go to law school that year, this was my *dream job.*

Felicia was the Latina policy expert I wanted to be. It would be too simple to say that she inspired me just because she was Latina. She inspired me because she was unapologetically Latina.

I thought being a woman in politics meant dressing in boring clothes that made you look more professional (in other words, whiter). Felicia taught me that wasn't true.

I thought being a woman in politics meant straightening my long curly hair to look more professional (also . . . whiter). Felicia taught me that wasn't true.

I thought being a woman in politics meant people would eventually come to accept you as being the person in charge. Felicia taught me that wasn't true.

Even though she was a lawyer with two Ivy League degrees and was leading the way on comprehensive immigration reform, people would often greet Felicia awkwardly because they were surprised that someone like her could have that much power and responsibility. But Felicia never skipped a beat or let these moments overshadow her work. She stayed unapologetically who she was.

In Felicia, I saw myself, and I realized that my Mexican American background did not have to be something I simply tolerated; it was something I could fully embrace in the workplace.

★ ★ ★

In April 2013, I left my position at USCIS and started my new job on the White House Domestic Policy Council's immigration team. Unlike a lot of my friends, I didn't start at the actual White House complex. I started in the Vice President's office in the Dirksen Senate Office Building, room 201. At first, it was just the four of us: Esther, Felicia, Tyler, and me. We were special envoys from the White House, fighting for President Obama's vision of the bill and communicating the bill's progress to the West Wing every single day. It was our job to make sure that the President's policy positions were reflected in Senate bill S.744. Dirksen 201 was the nerve center, and we were the brain of the operation, pulling strings behind the scenes.

For this bill to be a success and become a law, it had to pass several obstacles.

1. The Senate Judiciary Committee would conduct a "markup" of the bill, which meant that any senators on the committee could offer amendments to change the original Gang of Eight bill. Then, if a majority of the committee voted in favor of the bill, it would go to the full Senate for debate and more amendments.
2. If the bill passed the Senate with enough votes, it would be sent to the House of Representatives for committee consideration, full House debate, and vote.

3. If both the House and the Senate voted in favor of the bill, it would go through a conference process, where members of the House and Senate gather to reconcile any differences between the two versions of the bill.

4. Finally, if both the Senate and the House voted in favor of the reconciled version of the bill, it would go to President Obama for his signature, which would mark the bill's official transformation into law.

Simply put, this bill had to go through a long and difficult journey to actually become law. There had not been a major immigration reform bill passed in my lifetime (the last one had been signed into law in 1986). While there were other immigration-related bills passed in the nineties, none of them reformed the entire system. As a student of past immigration legislation, I knew we had a monumental challenge before us—but if we passed this bill, we would be part of history.

On the first day of the Senate Judiciary Committee markup, around five p.m., amendments started coming in via email from senators on the committee, people I had been following in the news for years—senators like Ted Cruz, Jeff Sessions, Dick Durbin, and Dianne Feinstein. We had to not only read and understand each amendment's content but develop a policy position on each as well.

I was in charge of managing the nerve center at Dirksen by creating an organizational system for all the policy we had to analyze. But unlike a lot of jobs, work at the White House doesn't include training. All I had was Felicia's vote of confidence that I could do this, and in that moment, that had to be enough. I felt a tidal wave of responsibility and complex policy hit me all at once. How does one create a simple system for a policy issue as complicated as immigration law?

And that's when Esther came roaring into my life.

I learned quickly that Esther Olavarria was one of the greatest immigration experts of our time (of all time, probably). On that first night in the nerve center, Esther stood patiently by my side and talked me through every amendment with her characteristically calm voice. Even though she had been in this field for decades, she was ready to teach me the basics. She was small like me, soft-spoken, and serious, but she exuded an almost tangible warmth and wisdom.

Before meeting Esther, I used to think that power meant taking up the most space in the room—that successful people in politics had to sacrifice kindness and decency to be effective. But Esther taught me that you can be incredibly kind and still hold power. It wasn't uncommon for senators to barge into the nerve center, asking for Esther's advice. She had been working on immigration policy in the Senate for over a decade, and they knew she had all the answers.

Even though she was practically a celebrity in DC, Esther was the exact opposite of every showboat man I'd encountered in politics—and this discovery delighted me.

During markup, my job was to oversee the daily happenings of the nerve center, coordinate with agency experts who were on call to answer any questions, and wait for policy questions from my team, who spent each day in the committee room negotiating directly with senators and their staff. Once I received a request through text or email, I had at most two minutes to make sure Felicia, Esther, and Tyler had the right answer before the wrong language (such as a change that would make it harder for certain immigrants to come to the United States) made its way into the bill. Sometimes I would have to run down the hallway to get them information in time because we couldn't wait for an attachment to send via email.

With Esther's guidance, I got better at my job. She helped me understand that even my role as the most junior staffer in the nerve center was critical to our ability to pass the best piece of legislation possible. I learned that contributing to political change not only means working incredibly hard and learning from your mistakes the first time; it also means taking care of your team members in unexpected ways—like figuring out how everyone takes their coffee, what time the café serves fresh popcorn, and that wine at five p.m. improves everyone's mood during a long workday. Most importantly, I learned that the most crucial change makers were not always going to be the people I read about in the news, but sometimes people like us, staffers behind the scenes.

Our thirteen- to fifteen-hour days were punctuated by updates to Cecilia Muñoz, the head of the Domestic Policy Council. Cecilia was one of the women-of-color policy experts President Obama hired to serve in his senior staff at the White House. While she was responsible for advising him on policy issues ranging from rural affairs to health care, she spent twenty years before the White House working as an immigration advocate. Cecilia was Felicia's boss, which meant that I was working for some of the most inspiring Latinas in the country.

The nerve center was truly the locus of activity for the immigration bill. You never knew who might walk in. Sometimes it was a senator, sometimes it was a Cabinet Secretary, and sometimes it was a famous person I didn't even recognize. Over time, the media set up cameras outside 210 to capture the people coming in and out of the room. One day, a picture of Esther trying to sneak in discreetly showed up on the front page of the *New York Times*. It was typical Esther. She was trying to stay behind the scenes so the media would focus on the real issue at hand: fixing our broken immigration system.

The most memorable day of markup was the night the bill passed the Senate committee. The room where the committee met was packed with onlookers. I was sitting in the front row of the audience, next to Senator Richard Blumenthal, in a bright purple blazer (something I never would have worn before I met the White House immigration team), trying not to cry on national television as I watched the committee prepare to take a vote on the bill. Because some members of the Gang of Eight were on the committee, we knew it would pass this first obstacle, but it didn't make it less exciting to watch Senator Patrick Leahy say "It passes," breaking the nervous tension in the room. The audience erupted into chants of *Yes we can* and *Sí se puede.*

My team and I embraced in tears, joyful that we had helped pass the first step of a great bill. That night, I felt the energy of knowing we were on the brink of something historic.

At the victory party, at a seafood restaurant on the Hill, I finally relaxed a bit with Tyler Moran, the fourth member of our team (and the honorary white member). Tyler is the type of person everyone wants to grab a beer with, so I jumped at the chance to drink vodka tonics with her as we celebrated. Tyler had been working in the immigration reform movement for over ten years, and she taught me the importance of celebrating every milestone when you are fighting for change. Most of the people at the victory party were immigration advocates who'd seen the last immigration bill fail in 2007. That night, Tyler told me to celebrate hard, because advocacy is exhausting and every bit of progress deserves recognition.

After the committee markup, I had seen for myself that political power can be brown, female, and congenial as hell. I began to call us the Gang of Four—the White House women critical to the success of the Gang of Eight. We were done with the committee. It was time to face the full Senate.

By June, amendments were coming at us from all sides. The bill was now under review by all one hundred senators for amendments, debate, and a vote on final passage. Every day, I was the first to receive an email with the latest amendments to the bill before they were considered by the Senate. I would read and summarize them—more than three hundred!—in a master spreadsheet. It felt as if everything was going as planned: we were about to pass the most progressive immigration bill in history. It included the signature policy of Obama's reelection promise: a path to citizenship for undocumented immigrants who have been living and working in our country for decades.

As Tyler and I grew closer, she gave me the confidence to be unabashedly pro-immigrant and unafraid of Republicans. When I was still deciding whether to choose a career in politics from inside government, as a public servant, or outside government, as an advocate, Tyler showed me that you can effectively do both. Tyler was a true organizer who liked to rabble-rouse and protest with the best advocates out there. She was also a policy expert who taught me that being a staffer, while ideologically complicated, can be rewarding, because you have to work within the system with the hope that you will change it for the better.

As a staffer, your goal is to collaborate with people you admire and respect, but it is rare that you will ever work for someone you agree with one hundred percent of the time. I knew when I accepted my job at the White House that at some point, I would disagree with a policy that I *was working on,* but I didn't know how I would feel about it when the time came.

Going into my job at the White House, I knew that I disagreed with President Obama's policies regarding the U.S.-Mexico border. He believed that he could gain Republican support for a path to citizenship by increasing security on the border. I believed that Republicans would never be satisfied with the amount of security on the southern border, and that they would always regard it with suspicion because of their xenophobic extremism.

Immigration is a racially charged topic. It's about who comes into our country and who becomes American. Even though we are indisputably a nation of immigrants, many Americans dispute the idea that immigration should continue. Because of this, during the Senate debate, every amendment was high profile and controversial, but not every senator had an equal chance to influence the bill.

For example, if a senator was important to the passage of the bill—a Republican whose vote the White House needed in order to increase bipartisan support, for example—their amendment was taken seriously. A senator was also more likely to have an amendment considered if he or she was "senior" in the Senate.

At the time, one of the newest women-of-color senators was Mazie Hirono, the Democratic senator from Hawaii and the only naturalized immigrant in the entire Senate. Senator Hirono was the only senator at the time who had personally navigated the immigration system. She wrote an amendment to address the way the system uniquely burdens women trying to make it to the United States and had a network of support from women's advocacy groups around the country. But Hirono was considered a junior senator, low in the hierarchy of seniority. People wouldn't take her amendment seriously. She hadn't earned the right to speak on a high-profile piece of legislation. Her state and constituents wanted her to act, but being elected to office does not always guarantee that your voice will be heard.

Seeing Senator Hirono struggle was difficult, especially when one of the senior senators who frequently made his voice heard was Jeff Sessions of Alabama. Sessions was vehemently against everything the White House wanted for this bill. Almost every day, he would make a speech on the Senate floor railing against immigrants, using old racist language from the history books I used to read. Even though nobody was responding to him directly, his opposition influenced the major compromise that was brewing.

The leader of the Gang of Eight, Senator Chuck Schumer of New York, believed that the future of the bill was dependent on the number of Republicans who supported it. The logic was this: if Senate Republicans overwhelmingly supported the bill, there would be enormous pressure on the Speaker of the House, John

Boehner, to bring the bill to the full House of Representatives for a vote. As a result, any Republican who threatened to withhold their vote would have their amendment considered if it would increase the likelihood of their voting for the final legislation. Two of these senators were Bob Corker, a Republican from Tennessee, and John Hoeven, a Republican from North Dakota. Both men came from states with low populations of immigrants. Neither of them had personal experience navigating the immigration system. Yet somehow, these two men became integral to the future of S.744.

This didn't feel fair to me. I didn't want to accept that the future of this bill was in the hands of two men who might not intimately understand the personal stories of immigrants whose lives would be shaped by the legislation.

Before the hunt for Republican votes truly began, the Gang of Four was involved in almost every discussion. By mid-June, when negotiations with Corker and Hoeven started, we were often left in the dark, waiting for news that came out of rooms we weren't invited into. We heard only tidbits and rumors, nothing tangible. We knew, for example, that Mark Zuckerberg had become heavily involved in negotiating the future of immigrants in the tech industry. We knew that Senator Schumer was becoming obsessed with the number of Republicans he could convince to sign on, often at the expense of a progressive policy we had preserved during the committee process. And we knew Senator Bernie Sanders of Vermont was skeptical of immigration reform; he was worried about immigrants taking American jobs.

The result of these discussions would come in the form of one giant amendment that contained some but not all of the amendments we had reviewed. We didn't know when the final amendment would be completed, and we didn't know what it would say.

And then, on June 20, the amendment hit my in-box around six p.m. Its arrival set off a flurry of activity in the nerve center. First, my team and I turned to my massive amendment spreadsheet to determine which amendments had made it into the final compromise. Next, we called in extra help from the White House Office of Management and Budget to understand just how much this bill would cost. As the hours passed, more policy experts joined us to figure out exactly how this amendment impacted S.744. Senior staff at the White House had reservations about the amendment, but supported the compromise. This meant that whether we liked what we were reading or not, we would have to defend, explain, and support this amendment to immigration advocates, the media, and Senate staff who relied on us to better understand the proposed policy.

When I read the Hoeven-Corker amendment, one number stood out: forty thousand. The amendment to our bill proposed sending forty thousand more troops to the border region of the United States. This was the moment I had been dreading.

Like too many Latinx kids, I grew up scared of all immigration enforcement. Because unlike most of the people reading the amendment in Dirksen 210 that night, I was one of the few born and raised on the U.S.-Mexico border.

I knew what forty thousand more border patrol officers meant.

I remembered the day in seventh grade when my sixteen-year-old brother picked me up from school and made an illegal left turn. After he was pulled over by the police, we waited and waited for the officer to come talk to him. Instead, the officer called the border patrol, and my brother and I had to answer questions we weren't expecting: Were we citizens? Yes. Did I have an ID? No, I was twelve years old. What's that in your lap? A viola.

Neither of us understood why my father was so angry that night.

As I read the amendment, I knew that the presence of more officers on the border would impact not only immigrants but Latino families who call the border home—those of us who know that no matter how long our family has been in the United States, we will continue to be regarded with suspicion by law enforcement. Democratic leaders stomached this reality. They changed the entire nature of the bill from one that prioritized citizenship and immigrants to one that accepted the Republican Party's racialized view of our southern border.

There are moments in your twenties that obliterate your long-held beliefs. For me, one such moment came with the realization that there were limits to how much the Democratic Party would align with my values. The institutions you revere growing up sometimes disappoint you. When they do, you have two choices: give up on them and find inspiration elsewhere, or try to change them into the institution you hope they will be. I wouldn't always be successful in the latter, but I wouldn't feel satisfied with the former.

I knew the Hoeven-Corker amendment was a political compromise, and I knew that if President Obama truly had his way, we probably wouldn't be dealing with it. This was the first night I had to reckon with the fact that I was working for a president who was more moderate than I was. Whom I respected deeply, but who didn't see the same costs of the political concession as I did.

The next day, Senator Patrick Leahy of Vermont, a Democratic leader I deeply admired, released a statement that the Hoeven-Corker amendment was a disappointment to him and to many others but that legislating "is not about standing on the sidelines and complaining that you cannot get a perfect solution enacted."

I would have preferred a compromise that did not place more troops on the border, but like Senator Leahy, I would rather be working for President Obama, trying to secure a path to citizenship for undocumented immigrants, than doing anything else.

It will always be important to me that I tried to fix a broken system rather than give up because the vehicle for change wasn't perfect.

By the last week of June, the debate and amendments had ended, and the day came for the Senate to take a final vote on the new version of the bill, with the Hoeven-Corker amendment included.

One of the honorary men of the Dirksen 201 team was Ed Pagano, from the White House Office of Legislative Affairs. He was in and out of 201 for the entire three months of the Senate's consideration of the bill, wheeling and dealing with his former Senate colleagues and making sure there was always a bag of chocolate on hand. He announced that the Senate leadership had decided to take a final vote on the bill on June 27, which just happened to be my twenty-fifth birthday.

The morning of the vote was uncharacteristically quiet in Dirksen. We had counted the votes over and over again, and we knew this bill was going to pass. It was so guaranteed to pass that Vice President Biden chose to preside over the vote and Senate Majority Leader Harry Reid invoked a special rule that required every senator to sit at their desk and stand to orally give their vote—a rare event.

We didn't have much to do as we waited, so we went outside to see the Vice President's motorcade drive past, waving like the immigration-policy nerds we were.

When the time came for the final vote, I walked over with the Gang of Four while documentary filmmakers captured the moment. They had been following the immigration reform process since 2001 and wanted to film the passage of this historic immigration bill. It was such a powerful moment that we walked in silence the entire way.

We went up to the Senate viewing chambers and sat and watched as every senator stood to give an oral vote—yea or nay. Even though we knew the votes ahead of time, it felt momentous every time a hard-earned ally voted *yea*.

Finally, with the sound of Biden's gavel hitting the desk, the bill passed, 68 to 32.

Even though Senate rules prohibit making noise in the viewing chamber, everyone cheered. This was history, and no Senate rule could suppress the joy and relief in the room. From where I sat, I could see Adrian Saenz, the Latino political operative who gave me my first job, and Stephanie Valencia, a mentor who had known me since I was in diapers. I couldn't help but think of Robert Raben, who gave me a chance when I first moved to DC, and Ali Mayorkas, my former boss at USCIS. All of them reminded me that I was a small part of a much bigger movement of advocates who, like me, believe that the future of the Latinx community in the United States is inextricably linked to the future of immigrants in the United States.

I had felt out of place in politics since college, but at this moment, on this day, I knew I was exactly where I belonged.

★ ★ ★

We all went back to Dirksen 201. We read every news article analyzing the bill and its chances for success moving forward. Because of the differences in House rules, the fate of the bill was entirely in the hands of Speaker John Boehner. Unlike in the Senate, the only bills that reach the floor of the House are the ones that the speaker and his party want to vote on. We always knew it was possible that Boehner would refuse to consider S.744, but we kept hoping that the strength of the legislation would overcome our fear.

There was one common theme in the news stories: Boehner didn't want to touch the Senate bill. Unlike the Republicans in the Senate, the Republicans in the House didn't think the bill was tough enough on the border. Many released statements saying that the bill provided amnesty for illegal immigrants. Others promised they would *never* vote for a path to citizenship. Without the support of the Republican Party in the House, Boehner had little incentive to bring the bill up for a vote, and as time would reveal, he never did.

The journey of S.744 was over the day it began.

One of the happiest days of my career was also the saddest.

We know now that S.744 never made it to the House, much less to President Obama's desk. Even though we had made the enormous compromise of promising to put forty thousand troops on the border, no amount of harsh enforcement from Democrats would convince Republicans to pass an immigration bill.

As the news sank in, Felicia surprised me with a birthday cake. When times got dark, the immigration ladies were always there for each other. So we took tequila shots and ate white cake covered in strawberries.

And despite the news, we celebrated. Because no matter what happened after that day, on the afternoon of June 27, we'd made history.

On the day I turned twenty-five, I learned that making change through our political system is harder than I ever imagined. But in spite of this, I, *a woman of color in politics,* belong. From now on, when people question my ambition, when they ask me why I keep fighting for humane immigration policy, why I don't give in to anger, I will tell them the story of Esther, Tyler, and Felicia. I will tell them how we keep hoping, even when it feels like there is not enough hope to go around.

I will think of this day every year. Every birthday I will question whether what we did mattered. I know I will return to the Senate, to Congress. I will come back for the opportunity to pass another imperfect, complicated bill. I will not give up until we have finished the work that Esther started in the Senate decades ago, securing a path to citizenship for undocumented immigrants and modernizing our laws to preserve our legacy as a nation of immigrants. What keeps me going is thinking of Esther standing next to the President as she (and, hopefully, our next president is a she) signs the bill into law.

Change is not simple. It is not triumphant. Sometimes it comes in the form of failure. But every year I will remind myself that while we didn't succeed that day, I have faith that one day we will.

KALISHA DESSOURCES FIGURES

Title: Policy Advisor
Office: White House Council on Women and Girls
Age: 25
Date: June 14, 2016

Walter E. Washington Convention Center. Washington, DC.
June 14, 2016.

That day, I witnessed an incredible amount of magic.

Somehow, with shaky hands, sweaty palms, and indisputably
high nerves, I managed to get the words out:

"Mr. President, Ms. Gloria Steinem."

"Mr. President, Ms. Kerry Washington."

"Mr. President, meet our partners from Civic Nation. They
helped make today possible!"

Standing two and a half inches from the ground on wedged
heels I should have thought way more about wearing (you know,
the ones that look comfortable but totally are not) and sporting a
knee-length white dress that became "the one" at approximately
one-thirty that morning, I held a neatly stacked deck of white
index cards in my hand. Printed on each card was the name of the
person I was introducing to President Obama. He stood two feet

to my left, in front of a "United State of Women"–logoed back-drop perfect for photo-line picture snapping. He greeted each guest with a smile and a hug, and words of gratitude and appreciation for the work they were doing on the front line of gender equality each and every day.

But obviously, not Gloria's name, or Kerry's, or the wonder-ful team at Civic Nation that had worked tirelessly with Jordan Brooks and me to execute this event could have slipped my mind, even with the added nerves of addressing the President of the United States.

"Mr. President, Ms. Cecile Richards."

Backstage, I watched the utter joy on Oprah Winfrey's face as she embraced her mentee, Mpumi Nobiva, who would introduce both Ms. Winfrey and First Lady Michelle Obama in just a few hours. It was my first time seeing or meeting Ms. Winfrey, and my mind pulled me back to the many days after school that I'd lie sprawled out on the family room couch in the company of my mother, watching her talk show. See, Oprah meant something to women—to Black women—across the country. She expanded the notion of what was possible for us. She made us feel visible. And if I've learned anything in my twenty-eight years of life, it's that visibility is important.

As Oprah embraced Mpumi, you could feel the strength and genuineness of their relationship. This wasn't staged, or rehearsed, or for the cameras. With no one watching except flies on the wall (myself included), Oprah pressed her thumb to Mpumi's cheek to wipe away a blemish or makeup mishap, in much the same way a mother or auntie would do before church service. There was magic in that moment. And when Mpumi later took the stage, introducing two of the most influential Black women—and American women—this country had ever seen to an audience of six thousand, the magic continued. *Black-girl magic.*

And that Black-girl magic stayed strong all day. It's the brightest I've ever witnessed.

Then there was the pure rush of racing around the six hundred tables and thousands of guests at the convention center in a relentless effort to find the girls of Mathtastic 4 moments before their chance to meet Mrs. Obama. I was juggling a million things backstage, and typically, if a guest doesn't make it to the photo line on time, we just keep the show going. *But I couldn't.*

See, I remember the day I met the Mathtastic 4—a group of four Black girls from a Cleveland, Ohio, middle school. I'd watched them just one month prior at the MATHCOUNTS competition in Washington, DC. Part of my policy portfolio—or area of focus—involved identifying best practices for expanding access to STEM education for girls of color, and the MATHCOUNTS competition was a way for me to engage with key stakeholders on behalf of the White House.

All the competitors were impressive, but none more so than the Mathtastic 4. They tackled the topic of probability, counting, and combinatorics in an innovative way, producing a hilarious black-and-white silent film in which four senior citizens reenact going to the movies and figuring out how to sit in four seats so everyone would be happy. They lit up the stage, countering the all-too-common misconception that Black girls can't be math wonks and STEM pioneers.

A local Cleveland paper read:

> While at the competition, the girls were approached by Kalisha Dessources, Policy Advisor to the White House Council on Women and Girls, about coming back to Washington, DC, to present their video at the upcoming White House Summit on the United State of Women, which was the capstone conference on women and girls.

I had no idea where they would fit on our lengthy, packed agenda, but I knew I'd make it work somehow. For me, *there is always room for Black girls.* And I was determined to make the White House Summit on the United State of Women full of as much Black-girl magic as possible.

The day of the summit, I located them just in time. A combination of crossed emails and bad cell-phone service caused their delay. We raced through the backstage corridors, me in my white dress, them in their bright purple tutus, and finally saw Jordan standing two steps to the left of Mrs. Obama, white index cards in hand:

"Mrs. Obama, this is the Mathtastic 4!" Jordan said with excitement and relief. And their reaction in that moment—eyes wide, chunky tears running down cheeks, and fogged-up glasses—was pure, indescribable, joyous magic.

★ ★ ★

And then there was Mikaila Ulmer. Standing no more than four feet five inches tall and clocking in at just over eleven years on this earth, Mikaila was a proud entrepreneur—Founder and Chief Executive Officer of Me & the Bees Lemonade. Hailing from Austin, Texas, she had launched her lemonade business from her front yard and ambitiously worked to get the attention of millions. Just as Mikaila stood ready to head onstage for her very special introduction, President Obama walked up and stood right behind her. Sensing a presence, she turned and in an emotional outburst gasped, "Oh my gosh!" Jordan and I, along with the team of advancers, speechwriters, and White House Communications staff, stood back, pinned near the draped curtains that confined us in the backstage arena.

And in that moment I remembered the chain of emails. . . .

Subject: The President's introducer at the United State of Women.

A team of us from communications, speechwriting, and the Council on Women and Girls tossed around ideas about who would introduce the President at the United State of Women Summit, one of the biggest conferences to be organized at the Obama White House. The names of well-accomplished female CEOs, thought leaders, and activists all came up as valid and amazing suggestions.

And then came mine: eleven-year-old Mikaila Ulmer.

★ ★ ★

The image will never leave my mind: Mikaila, with flawless chocolate-brown skin and the big, quick tears that fell from her eyes. The smile on her face as she looked up to this six-foot African American man we each had the honor, and the privilege, and the incredible opportunity to call Mr. President. I promise you. It was magic. And to feel like part of crafting that magic—well, that was just indescribable.

★ ★ ★

The United State of Women Summit was the culmination of a journey that had had its first big moment 2,693 days before, in January 2009, when President Obama sat behind his desk in the Oval Office and signed into law the Lilly Ledbetter Fair Pay Act, a federal statute that would prevent pay discrimination for women. The act was named after a supervisor at the Goodyear Tire & Rubber Company who, after nineteen years of hard work, learned that she was making thousands of dollars less per year than male colleagues in the same position. It was the first bill signed into law by President Barack Obama, and it foreshadowed what would become an eight-year commitment to making this country more equitable for women from every community.

On the day of the summit, I said calmly and confidently as I neared the end of my stack of index cards:

"Mr. President, Ms. Lilly Ledbetter."

Two months after the Lilly Ledbetter Act became law, in March 2009, President Obama signed an executive order to create the White House Council on Women and Girls—an interagency council that ensured that every Cabinet Secretary, federal agency, and White House department across the federal government applied a lens of gender equity to every policy and program they created. I was eighteen when President Obama signed that executive order, a freshman at Cornell University, declaring a minor in feminism and gender studies and planning to embark on research into the sad state of paid parental leave policy in the United States.

And there I was: one of two White House staffers tasked with running the everyday operations of the White House Council on Women and Girls and telling the story of its legacy through this enormous summit. We had 267 speakers from every community, industry, background, and walk of life and 6,000 advocates and activists from every corner of the country; they tackled issues including women's health, entrepreneurship, criminal justice reform, education, and civic engagement. We had one president, one vice president, one first lady.

But what a journey it was to the magic of that day. It was not without its twists and turns. Jordan and I laughed, and cried, and worried. We hardly slept, and on too many evenings we justified an order of sweet potato fries from the West Wing Navy Mess as an adequate, well-balanced meal. We surprised each other and ourselves. With all the ups and the downs, *we made something.* And it was the result of the womanpower of a team of dedicated, brilliant folks who spanned the federal government—every agency, every White House shop. It was the result of a valiant effort by our incredible team and our nonprofit partners at Civic

Nation, led by Taylor Barnes and Ariana Heifetz; our operations queen, Ximena Gonzalez; and our rock-star intern, Evie Freeman. It was the vision and dedication of Valerie Jarrett and Tina Tchen, our forever-fearless leaders and everyday bosses.

But every big operation has a nucleus, a pulse, a heartbeat. That place where the fine-tuned details and logistics are hashed out, the problems are solved (or not), the good news comes in, and the bad news falls hard. While the White House Summit on the United State of Women was a complexity of moving pieces, its brainpower and heartbeat could be found at 1650 Pennsylvania Avenue NW, floor 2, suite 115, the second door from the left, where poster paper and Post-it notes spanned the entire wall; where color-coded star stickers marked every confirmed speaker; where stacks of meeting agendas covered ancient, hefty wood desks; and where two White House staffers with roles and responsibilities bigger than they could imagine burned the midnight, midmorning, and Saturday-afternoon oil.

So let's rewind. The road to magic . . .

The long journey to that day—being a policy advisor at the White House, being put in charge of an immense, groundbreaking event—certainly wasn't straightforward or clean-cut. That job, that opportunity, it was not locked down with the snap of a finger. Far from it. No one opened a door for me. But I relentlessly kept knocking.

See, I was never a political person (at least, I didn't think so). I cared enormously about issues of equity and access and opportunity. I'd always had a keen sense of what justice looked like and felt like. And as the daughter of Haitian immigrants whose life journeys were built on a tireless fight for opportunity and access, it was hard to imagine myself pursuing any path in life that—at its core—did not entail the constant pursuit of more fairness, more equity, and more opportunity.

"That's not fair!" I'd cry all the time growing up.

"That's your favorite thing to say," my mom would tease. "'That's not fair!'" she'd say, mocking me. "What's not fair?"

And yes, at age eight, my constant complaint that "that's not fair" was less likely a stance on social justice and equity than a campaign against some scenario in which one of my three sisters got something I did not. But I promise, it grew into something far greater.

As I said, I was never a political person, but I remember that feeling I had after Trayvon Martin was killed in his South Florida neighborhood by a man who was supposed to protect and ensure safety for his community. I remember the anxiety I felt when I understood the way my students at the all-boys high school where I once taught navigated their communities in Philadelphia—communities with high rates of gun violence, underresourced schools, limited access to health care, wages that simply weren't enough to get by. I remember constantly feeling that *That's not fair*—the odds were stacked against them in a way that was untenable.

And I remember the feeling of deep curiosity when I watched President Obama on television, giving remarks to launch his My Brother's Keeper Initiative, which was focused on opportunity and outcomes for boys and young men of color. The President recounted stories of young men he had met in the South Side of Chicago—their obstacles, challenges, and experiences. Well, those young men were my students. My Brother's Keeper was an initiative *for them.* And thus began my obsession with understanding how policy trickles down from the White House pressroom to the communities and individuals it was actually made for. I did not then know how, but I knew I wanted to be in those conference rooms in Washington, helping to figure it out.

★ ★ ★

Well, my first-ever email from the White House read something like this:

> Dear Applicant: Thank you for applying to the Summer 2013 White House Internship Program. We regret to inform you that we are unable to offer you an internship at this time.

I made progress by the summer of the following year. My email this time from the vague "White House Internship Application" address concluded with:

> We are not able to offer you an internship at this time, but we would like to place you on our wait list in case an opportunity becomes available.

And just months later, in the fall, I finally got the email that I knew was meant for me:

> Dear Applicant: We are pleased to inform you that you have been accepted to participate in the Fall 2014 White House Internship Program.

You know that thing they say about the third time? But this was more than just a charm.

See, I looked up to, admired, and wanted to be part of the legacy of a man who, in the spring of 2000, waged an unsuccessful attempt at a seat in Illinois's First Congressional District, bringing in just 30 percent of the vote. A man who four years later claimed a seat in the U.S. Senate and eight years later made history as the first Black President of the United States.

If Barack Obama could throw himself back in the ring after rejection and defeat, well, so could I. And I did. And if the third time had not been a charm, there would have been a fourth. Rejection is good, and it's healthy, and it's part of the journey that will make you who you are. So keep knocking.

In August 2014, I packed a car's worth of belongings, found a Craigslist sublease, and headed to Washington, DC, to intern at the White House for Heather Foster and Ashley Allison, the President's liaisons to the African American and faith-based communities, respectively. *Black women.* In them, I saw myself. And because of them, I learned a lesson or two, or twenty, about what it means to find success in a place like the White House. They expanded my notion of what was possible for me.

It was an incredible five months. It was a tough five months. I swiped out of the White House complex at ten p.m. on most days. I was afraid of making mistakes. I was reluctant to take up space. But I worked feverishly, because this president, my students—the things I believed in—made it all worthwhile.

One day during the final weeks of my internship, Yohannes

Abraham, Chief of Staff to Valerie Jarrett, the President's Senior Advisor and Chair of the White House Council on Women and Girls, summoned me to his office. He told me I'd been asked to interview for a full-time assistant role with the Office of Inter-governmental Affairs (IGA). My job would be to support the IGA team in managing the President's communications, correspon-dence, and relationships with our nation's governors and state elected officials. As Yohannes explained the role, I counted in my head the number of governors I knew by name. "Andrew Cuomo, Chris Christie . . ." I was a New Yorker, clearly.

But wait . . . did you catch that?

After five months of interning, at the age of twenty-four, I was asked to interview for a *real job* at the White House. Work-ing for President Barack Hussein Obama. But I wasn't sure I'd be good at it. Was I politically savvy enough? Did I understand the intricacies of how laws were passed in state legislatures? For this twenty-four-year-old Black girl, the world of governors—which in 2014 was overwhelmingly male and overwhelmingly white—seemed . . . well, it seemed foreign at best. But in the nine months I spent in that role (Yes! I got it!), I made room for myself.

Nine months later, Yohannes pulled me into his office in much the same way.

"I want you to sit down with Valerie and Tina," he said. "Kim Leary is leaving, and we want to do some restructuring of the Council on Women and Girls."

I was unsure of how I'd fit into that restructuring. Dr. Kimber-lyn Leary, a University of Michigan–minted PhD and a profes-

sor at Harvard, had spent the past year as a fellow in the White House creating a new policy portfolio that focused on the unique needs, challenges, and obstacles faced by women and girls of color across the country.

I was three years removed from college, with an enormous passion for racial and gender equity . . . but, come on, I was still on my dad's health insurance plan (#Obamacare). On a good day, I felt marginally like an actual adult. Managing a portfolio at the *White House,* for *this* president? It seemed unreal.

But see, this wasn't an isolated situation. I was part of a larger priority of the Obama White House. The President, the First Lady, Valerie, Tina, and other senior staff had a deep trust in young staffers. They valued our passionate minds. Our relentless hope. Our millennial perspectives. Our energy—the kind of energy that would shake things up. Across the board, they took risks on us.

And so I headed into the interview I had been simultaneously awaiting and fearing for the entirety of that week.

"Do you have any questions for me about the role?" Tina Tchen, Chief of Staff to the First Lady and Executive Director of the White House Council on Women and Girls, asked me as I sat in her polished East Wing office.

"What are some projects you see on the horizon?" I asked.

She replied that she wanted to do something *big,* something cumulative, something that could really show the legacy of gender-equity work across the two terms of President Obama's Administration.

What would soon become the White House Summit on the United State of Women was still a vague concept. But the broader vision? Tina saw it along.

Something big, I'd thought. My mind raced back to the many events that I had planned and executed as a White House intern and staff assistant. I had the calculations down to a science: 180 guests in South Court Auditorium meant we could plan on an invite list near 220. I had the template for a perfectly designed agenda, to be sent to the print shop the evening before an event. I knew exactly how many boxes of White House chocolates to order to ensure there was one for each guest as they departed the auditorium to head toward the exit gates of the White House complex. I knew the best breakout session rooms for small discussions, the best protocol for handling a VIP guest, the best menu options for a catered lunch from Ike's.

I could do big.

But what Tina had in mind was certainly much bigger than I could have imagined at that moment.

Days after interviewing with Tina, I sat adjacent to Valerie Jarrett on the sleek couch in her West Wing office. As a staff assistant, my face time with Valerie was slim. I didn't meet with her regularly—my bosses did—and the few minutes when I'd get a glimpse of her in action weren't enough to know what to expect from an interview with her. Of course, I prepared for the worst: to be grilled on every legislation and policy that involved women and girls. To give recommendations on how to improve access to capital for women and paid parental leave policies.

But Valerie's approach that day was completely unexpected.

"So what's important to you?" she asked.

We landed on a conversation about my three incredible sisters, my love for education policy, and my concern for the realities I saw as a middle and high school teacher in North and West Philadelphia—realities for students of color who looked like me. I learned quickly that was who Valerie was: a fierce leader and a high-expectations boss, but at her core, a person with a deep concern for what drove people in the work they did. That was how she built the team around her. Those qualities are what strengthened the legacy of the Administration.

It's no wonder Valerie sought to build a team with someone like Jordan Brooks.

I remember the first time I met Jordan, my partner in crime in all things. And I mean *all things.* She had a collection of scarf-blanket hybrids she wore wrapped around her shoulders, over a perfect collection of career dresses. I hadn't known her name before, but I knew she was the right-hand woman to Tina Tchen, and when I asked a colleague what her role was, he replied, "Oh, she knows *all* the lady things." That she did.

Jordan too was in job limbo. She started as a White House staffer in the photo office in 2009, after working on the President's campaign in south Virginia. She was twenty-two.

She'd spent years in that role, eventually moving on to be Tina Tchen's Special Assistant, then Assistant Director to the White House Council on Women and Girls, and now she also was having conversations with Valerie and Tina as part of this "restructuring" that Yohannes had mentioned. On the table for her: being the Deputy Executive Director of the Council on Women and Girls.

Catching Jordan for a moment one day at the base of the EEOB's Navy Steps on West Executive Avenue, I asked her if she had heard any news or updates after her interviews with Tina and Valerie. She hadn't. Eyes bright with curiosity, she asked if I had heard anything, and I shared the same.

"You think they'll let us run this thing?" she said with widened eyes and a smile, a look of Jordan's that I would soon get to know pretty well.

It was a wild idea. She and I would be barely twenty-nine and barely twenty-five (our birthdays, coincidentally, are on the same day), coordinating the White House's policy and public engagement shop on all things women and girls. We would be responsible for managing an interagency council tasked with ensuring that all the policy and programs that came out of the White House and federal government had a clear consideration for the gender inequality that still exists across institutions and systems. We would manage communications with some of the biggest, fiercest leaders of the women's rights and gender-equity community—the Cecile Richardses, Melanie Campbells, Fatima Goss Graveses, Gloria Steinems, Angela Glover Blackwells, and Ellie Smeals of the world.

Jordan and I both knew it was possible, but it still seemed so far-fetched.

"They should just let us run this thing," she concluded.

Well—*they did.*

I heard from Yohannes a few weeks later, and the journey began. Kalisha Dessources, age twenty-five, Policy Advisor to the White House Council on Women and Girls, now owned the portfolio on advancing equity for women and girls of color.

★★★

My portfolio was deeply personal to me.

When White House policy wonks discussed the realities of unplanned and teen pregnancy, and how it disproportionately impacts girls and young women of color, it hit home. I remember Rebecca, a bright African American girl in my eighth-grade class, who was the mother of a one-year-old boy. I remember Rebecca's defeated look when I passed her desk and set eyes on her incomplete fractions homework. Being a young mom while finishing middle school without adequate resources—that was a steep mountain to climb.

In 2016, our team convened a daylong conference to discuss trauma-informed approaches to school discipline policies with superintendents, Secretaries of Education, and policy professionals from across the country. This conference was also incredibly personal to me. See, I've taught at schools where zero-tolerance discipline policies prevailed. I've watched my students be repeatedly suspended, expelled, and pushed into alternative education placements where a culture of militarization superseded their scholarly pursuits . . . for infractions that were harmless, and part of their development as youth. I remember Cierrah, whose outbursts and anger sometimes got her dismissed from classrooms. What I knew was that Cierrah was actually coping with her father's death. What I knew was that Cierrah was one of the brightest, most confident, most innovative twelve-year-olds I had ever known. At the conference, Cierrah was my speaker of choice.

Talking about the policy that shaped the lives of girls of color with policy experts and government personnel, well, that just wasn't enough. Because the policy was tied to a Rebecca and to a Cierrah. So, shortly into my role, I vowed that the best way to move the work forward was to get as many girls of color through those White House gates as possible. And I did.

Sometimes they came by the tens, and sometimes by the hundreds—to discuss juvenile justice reform, to share their challenges with access to STEM education, to build robots, to code. . . .

Sometimes they came to dance for the First Lady.

"Well, I can be President now," I overheard an eight-year-old Black girl say boldly as I waited for her and her friend to change in the bathroom before their performance for the First Lady.

That day—perhaps one of my favorite at the White House—staffer Stephanie Young led the charge in organizing a Black History Month event. She brought in Black girls from every corner of Washington, DC, for master lessons with dance legends: Fatima Robinson, Debbie Allen, Judith Jamison. Then they performed for the First Lady.

And there was something about walking through the doors of the White House, about spending the day in the East Wing, about meeting the First Lady, that expanded the vision these girls had for themselves.

"We can both be President," her friend in the stall beside her replied.

You have to see yourself there to see yourself there.

★ ★ ★

Black-girl magic was present in all corners of the White House, from the East Wing to West Wing, and up all four flights of spiral steps in the Eisenhower Executive Office Building. Valerie Jarrett was one of the President's top aides and confidantes. Susan Rice kept us safe from national security threats. Deesha Dyer planned state dinners from the ground up. Heather Foster and Stephanie Young kept the first African American President of the United States connected to the African American and civil rights communities. Monique Dorsainvil kept the Office of Public Engagement running smoothly. Crystal Carson, Ashley Etienne, Desiree Barnes, and Addie Whisenant were all things press and White House communications. Karen Evans and Sarah Rutherford liaised with Cabinet Secretaries, and Rochelle Briscoe directed the process of presidential appointees. Ashley Allison and Shelly Marc strategized how we'd tackle engagement around criminal justice reform. There was Wintta Woldemariam in White House Counsel, and Adrienne Harris with the National Economic Council.

And of course, there was the First Lady of the United States herself, Black-girl magic personified. And there was me: a semi-adult with a relentless passion for public service and a route to the White House that I could never have dreamed up.

Every office, every corner, every team. The brightest minds and fiercest work ethic. Stories of struggle and obstacles, and perseverance, and success. Stories of Black-girl magic.

It's easy to forget how unique this was, the visibility and leadership of Black women in the White House. But in rewinding the clock sixty, twenty, even ten years back and remembering the days when those same halls were walked almost exclusively by white men . . . well, tracing that trajectory always reminded me that the Obama White House's Black-girl magic was a really big deal.

And the White House Summit on the United State of Women

was the culmination of it all. It was a slate of nine hours to show the progress made and the road ahead for women from every community. It was the chance to prove that the women's movement, while I had admired it from its very first days, was different now. It was centered on the voices and experiences and leadership and power of women and girls of color, who for far too long had been left out. It was intersectional, and diverse, and inclusive.

By February 2016, we were knee-deep in summit planning. Every day was a new challenge, a new hurdle, a new small win, a new journey—full of peaks and pits, and moments of complete adrenaline rush.

A pit like an email subject along the lines of "Scheduling Conflict: POTUS in Asia."

As a White House staffer, you learn very quickly to roll with the punches. By the time we received this email in March, we were already entrenched in summit logistics. The body of the email explained that the President, on the very day of our summit, *had* to take a trip to Vietnam. You know, world affairs.

I remember blocking off an entire evening weeks before to meticulously send out our speaker invitations and ticket allotments. I wanted the invitations to feel personal; a blast email just wasn't enough. And after taking some time to absorb the blow (fifteen minutes, at most), Jordan and I were right back in our sent boxes, going email by email, replying all and explaining that the entire event had to be moved. Putting out a fire. It's what we did. Remember, we were part of something bigger.

And there was no greater peak than the words "We've got

OPRAH!!!!" Jordan exclaimed it loud enough for the entire corridor of the Eisenhower Executive Office Building to hear as she hung up the phone with Amy Weinblum, Ms. Winfrey's Chief of Staff. Because getting on Oprah Winfrey's calendar is no small feat. Need I say more?

As for adrenaline, well, there's no rush quite like the first time you're asked to brief the First Lady of the United States.

It was supposed to go like this:

9:00 a.m.: Run-through at the convention center—a slot that left just enough time to make it back for an 11:00 a.m. briefing with Mrs. Obama.

But ended up going like this:

9:40 a.m.: Email To: Jordan Brooks and Kalisha Dessources From: Blaine Boyd, Staffer to the First Lady

Can we push up your briefing with FLOTUS? Can you guys head over in twenty minutes?

We totally couldn't. Neither of us was wearing shoes that day that could get us down New York Avenue, across Fifteenth Street, through security, and into the East Wing in eighteen minutes flat.

Reply All: We'll be right over.

Uber. No. Cab. Credit card. Swipe. Run.

Through security, up East Executive Avenue, into the East Wing, up the steps, turn right, turn right.

Though the odds were against us, we made it just in time . . . to wait thirty minutes for the First Lady of the United States. Again, we were part of something bigger.

There I sat, in the East Wing, with my legs crossed, wearing a high-collared yellow dress that I chose specifically in an effort to channel my inner Michelle Obama. Twenty-five years old, briefing the First Lady of the United States on the interview she'd do with Oprah Winfrey onstage at the United State of Women Summit. Looking square into the eyes of a woman whose complexion matched my own and whose hair curled up just the same way in summer heat. With Jordan Brooks to my left, and Tina Tchen to my right—two women who could have totally taken this meeting on their own, but who, in my entire time working with and for them, had always made room for me. The culmination of all those things? Magic.

And those same peaks, pits, and rushes of adrenaline . . . well, they carried forth to game day.

★ ★ ★

You know that feeling you get before the first day of school, or the first day at work in a new gig? The restless night of butterflies—or dragonflies—keeping you up? I never had that feeling more than the night before the summit.

My apartment's nine-hundred-square-foot floor was draped with three aligned air mattresses populated with my sleeping sisters and cousins who'd driven to Washington, DC, to be a part of the team of over one hundred volunteers. They were exhausted, rightfully so, after spending hours at the convention center that day assembling centerpieces for tables, and gift bags for participants. On the one vacant love seat, I had three dresses laid out—one red, one white, one blue. I had settled on matching the patriotic theme of the United State of Women—a name that Jordan and I and our team of creative partners had spent weeks racking our brains over—but was unsure which portion of the flag would be right for the day.

I scanned my White House BlackBerry over and over again

for any last-minute changes. I reviewed the run of show; triple-checked that I had direct contact lines to all of our speakers and backstage guests; quadruple-checked that we had properly vetted anyone who would be close to the President and the First Lady.

At 5:00 a.m., I called myself an Uber, leaving my army of a family behind to sleep for another hour or two before being on their feet for what would undoubtedly be a long day.

My mood shifted consistently between anxiety and complete and utter fear, but once I made it through those convention center doors and saw my partner in crime, Jordan, well, I knew that whatever the day brought us, we were prepared for it.

At 8:00 a.m., the program began. There was no turning back. No room for last-minute fixes. It was game time.

I learned very quickly that no matter how meticulous you are—detailing the run of show down to the very minute—the show never goes quite as planned. And it didn't.

Vice President Joe Biden is one of my heroes. Every time he speaks, I'm reminded of why I belong in public service. One of the youngest people ever to be elected to the Senate, he has spent his career championing a number of different issues. I knew him most affectionately as a fierce advocate on the forefront of combating violence against women—and that's what he took the stage to speak about so eloquently that day.

His remarks were never high level, or vague, or scripted. Sure, he had an excellent staff who helped him sum up his thoughts into formal remarks, but he rarely ever read from those memos. His remarks were personal, and real, and heartfelt. They mobilized people and communities and called attention to issues that are tough to discuss. I stood backstage that day, eyes glued to the TV projecting the onstage activity. "This is incredible," I thought.

Glancing down at my phone moments later, I saw that we were a very impressive forty-five minutes behind schedule.

"No big deal," you might think. But with logistics for six thousand guests, and the hard-line schedules of the President, the First Lady, Oprah Winfrey, Warren Buffett . . . huge deal. And at approximately 10:00 a.m., the fun *really* began: the day became filled with obstacles, challenges, on-the-spot strategizing, catching up, reworking, x-ing out, and scribbling in. The first few hours mimicked our perfectly planned agenda, and everything thereafter—well, that was improv. Starring yours truly: Kalisha and Jordan.

Remember when I said there was no room for last-minute fixes? At the White House, there's *always* room for last-minute fixes.

By 11:00 a.m., we knew we'd have one more speaker onstage: Attorney General of the United States Loretta Lynch. She was originally scheduled to be overseas but canceled that trip with little notice to be present and engaged, and to address a hurting nation after the tragedy at Pulse nightclub in Orlando, which happened just days before the summit. It didn't matter how tight the schedule was; this moment was undoubtedly the most important of the day. I remember getting the signal from our stage director that we needed Attorney General Lynch onstage in just three minutes. The AG was nowhere in sight. I peeked down at my cell phone to read a text update from my inside source,

Shomari Figures, White House Liaison to the Department of Justice, my then partner and now husband. It read: "She hasn't left the Department of Justice yet...."

We stalled the show for a total of fifteen minutes, which felt more like forty. When the Attorney General finally made it to the stage, when we observed a moment of silence in memory of those who had lost their lives during the Pulse nightclub shooting, I remembered how important this day was. Because the women's movement—the one pressed forward by the Obama Administration—was a movement against injustice everywhere. It was a movement *for* immigration reform, *for* criminal justice reform, *for* LGBTQ rights, *against* senseless gun violence. And the six thousand women and allies in that room? We needed every single one of them on the forefront. Jordan and I, email by email, had brought them there that day.

I caught my breath, and with a renewed sense of purpose and confidence that I could make it through the day, I scanned through my BlackBerry once more. That was when I saw this:

"Oprah's delayed.... Issue with plane..."

Yeah, that one felt important.

Despite the many hiccups, the bumps, and the frantic fixing, *the whole day was magic*. It was magic for Oprah, and for Kerry, and for Mikaila Ulmer. It was magic for the Mathtastic 4, fully decked out in their green spandex and purple capes. It was magic because of the Gloria Steinems and Cecile Richardses who have moved us one step closer to gender equality in this country. Magic for the Black girls, the DREAMers, the LGBTQ youth who never thought that places like the United State of Women were for them. Magic because of Dr. Carol Brown, on the forefront of fighting cancer for women; because of eleven-year-old Marley Dias, on the fore-front of making Black girls visible in books; because of Monique Morris, on the forefront of justice and equity in education.

But today was also magic because of me, a twenty-five-year-old with Haitian roots who was advancing and institutionaliz-ing the legacy of the President of the United States. And if it was magic because of me, it was magic because of Charlotte.

Charlotte Posy was thirty-five years old when she immigrated to the United States. Leaving her three daughters—Yole, Katlyn, and Yasmine—behind in Haiti, she boarded a plane bound for John F. Kennedy airport with a suitcase full of clothes, the work visa she needed, and nothing else to her name. Her journey was one of resilience, of hope, and, as a mother leaving behind those who mattered most, of deep pain and uncertainty. For her, the United States meant opportunity. It meant the ability to provide for her daughters. It meant high-quality education, economic security, sound health care, mobility—things she did not have access to.

Charlotte arrived in a small, immigrant-filled neighborhood in East Flatbush, Brooklyn, in 1970. She began her job as a factory seamstress, many days pulling upward of twelve-hour shifts. A single mother, it was up to her to give Yole, Katlyn, and Yasmine the opportunity they deserved. Three years later, after having worked, and saved, and worked, and saved, Charlotte sent for her daughters to join her in the United States.

My mother was one of those daughters, and she fought against the odds every single day. After immigrating to the United States, she arrived at her public school in East Flatbush, a place that was completely unfamiliar to her, wearing patent-leather shoes and lace-trimmed white socks. Speaking the tiniest amount of English, she struggled day after day to convince her peers and her teachers that she was capable and competent and intelligent. But my mom persevered.

And so the summit's magic went beyond just me. It was magic because I am the granddaughter of Charlotte and the daughter of Katlyn and my roots belong to a tiny island called Hispaniola. As I swiped through my deck of white cards, two steps to the left of the President of the United States, I was reminded with certainty that I wouldn't have this story to tell if not for Charlotte's journey, her bravery, her grit. It was magic because never could Charlotte have imagined as she boarded her plane, scared and alone, as she worked around the clock to save and to make a better life for her girls, that a place like the White House could be part of her family's story. There was no piece of Charlotte who would have believed that, in her own lifetime, she'd see her granddaughter walk the halls of the West Wing, brief the First Lady of the United States, or write memos for the President. You see, as a woman from an immigrant community, you are constantly challenged about whether this country belongs to you. Whether you can shape it, and mold it, and lead it. That day, I made clear to my grandmother that America was hers.

★ ★ ★

I'm appreciative of so many things. The opportunity to have been a part of crafting the United State of Women, and of showcasing the legacy of President and Mrs. Obama's fight for gender equality. I'm appreciative of my journey to that day. I'm appreciative of the strength of my mother and my grandmother, of the leadership of Tina and Valerie, and of every colleague across the federal government who responded to our requests for conference calls, meetings, and data to fold into the six policy reports we released in conjunction with the event.

And I'm appreciative of that tiny office on the second floor of the Eisenhower Executive Office Building, Suite 115, second door from the left, where I sat—sometimes at ease, but mostly amid rapid-fire emails and phone calls, obstacles and exhilaration—finding room for my feet on top of the mountain of shoes under my desk (it's a White House thing). I sat across from my partner in crime, Jordan—blanket-scarf tucked into the back of her chair, coffee mugs from every day of the week half-filled. I'm appreciative of her—my colleague, my mentor, and now one of the most incredible friends I could ask for in life.

The summit was about the President of the United States, our incredible First Lady, our champion of a Vice President. It was about the policy that made it through, and the policy that died in conference rooms across the White House. It was about the Susan B. Anthonys and the Rosa Parkses who paved the way for us to be here today. It was about a legacy, a story, and a call to action for the long journey ahead.

And in every room, and on every panel, it was about Black-girl magic.

TAYLOR LUSTIG

Title: Policy Assistant for White House Office of Faith-Based and
Neighborhood Partnerships
Office: Domestic Policy Council
Age: 25
Date: September 23, 2015

I flashed my badge through the iron bars of the north campus entrance, and the Secret Service agents poked their heads up with quizzical looks. I had been through these security gates thousands of times, but usually not this late at night, and never wearing my University of Texas Longhorn sweatpants.

I muttered a pathetic "Hiiiii" under my breath, swung my overnight bag onto the conveyor belt, and walked through the metal detector. The agent on duty took in my garb, the late hour, and my duffel and joked, "Aren't you going the wrong way, young lady?" I let out a "Ha!", grabbed my bag, and pushed through the door to the West Wing driveway, pausing just long enough to toss back a smile and a shrug. "Oh, you know, YOPO."

YOPO. As in You. Only. Pope. Once.

It was the night before the arrival ceremony of His Holiness Pope Francis on the South Lawn. Even by White House standards, this was a big deal. The number of people expected to pour into DC had led the district to shut down streets, issue alerts, reinforce security, and reroute metro cars. That meant that the only way I could be sure I'd actually get to the White House in time for the morning ceremony was to sleep there. The White House was planning to pack a record eleven thousand people onto the South Lawn, each of them holding the hottest ticket in town. This would be Pope Francis's first visit to the United States. In the two years since being elected, the Holy Father had captured the attention of people around the world, drawing crowds, galvanizing young people, and inspiring actions that echoed his core message: to better human life and strengthen the social and environmental structures that bind us together.

As I walked down the West Wing driveway and headed up the Navy Steps and into the Eisenhower Executive Office Building, the ground under my feet felt alive. The White House—the building itself—seemed to shimmer. I was a Policy Assistant in President Obama's Office of Faith-Based and Neighborhood Partnerships, a position I had started on Easter 2014. Whenever I was at the office at a late hour, I found myself awestruck by the place, aware of the incredible privilege and opportunity I had been given to make a difference. For the past seven months, I had been working on the pope's visit, ironing out the seemingly endless details that were required to bring the papal arrival ceremony to life. On the eve of that ceremony, all those hours of work felt like they had been transformed into raw energy. I couldn't imagine how I'd get any sleep that night, alone in my office—and I for sure couldn't imagine what the next twenty-four hours would bring.

Despite the late hour, the halls were brightly lit. To my surprise, I heard voices down the hallway of the first-floor south corridor. Apparently, I wasn't the only one nervous about getting here on time, looking to avoid the expected early-morning chaos on the streets. I dumped my overnight bag containing my work outfit, toothbrush, and mascara in my office and headed across the hall to join the slumber party.

So there I sat with a handful of coworkers atop desks and couches, everyone telling stories about their days. There was the usual late-night display of red Solo cups that accompanies a venting session about frustrating processes, last-minute schedule changes, or a visitor who got "stuck," or held up by Secret Service outside the security gates. We discussed projects people were working on, covering topics like criminal justice reform, health care, trade policy, and the refugee crisis in Syria. That was the beauty of conversation with my colleagues on the first floor of the Eisenhower Building—the variety. Across the Domestic Policy Council and the Office of Public Engagement, people were doing a million different things, making progress at a mile a minute, all with the same mission: to serve the President and his agenda. I was always learning about some new topic, new challenge, or new project from this diverse group of people who made up my work family, which deepened my understanding of policy making and often left me inspired. Some of us at the slumber party had been working on the papal visit, like the logistics for the morning arrival ceremony, but most people were staffers who had volunteered to be at work at the crack of dawn so they could witness this historic moment.

Suddenly, I realized it was midnight and I needed all the sleep I could get. We agreed on a wake-up time in the fours. It felt just like summer camp—the anticipation of the next day's activities, the camaraderie, and the team spirit—except instead of a cabin in the woods, I walked down a grand marble hallway to the women's restroom to brush my teeth.

I double-checked my alarms—I'd brought four of them—and shut the door to my office. I laid a throw blanket across the burgundy couch and propped up a pillow. Then I thought back to what had brought me to this day.

In March 2015, we started working with the Vatican's scheduling team and the U.S. Ambassador to the Holy See to determine when the pope would visit. After some back-and-forth, it was settled. His Holiness Pope Francis would formally arrive at the White House on September 23, 2015. It was the only date that worked for the Vatican, and it was Yom Kippur, the holiest day of the year in Judaism.

Even for someone Jew-ish like me, this presented a big conflict. If there was one thing I'd taken away from those long, dreaded hours I spent in Hebrew and Sunday schools, it was the importance of the High Holidays, a time that starts with the Jewish New Year and ends with Yom Kippur. Yom Kippur is the most solemn day of all, devoted to fasting and praying and repenting for sins.

If, like me, you were living in one of the predominantly Jewish suburbs of the North Shore of Chicago on Yom Kippur, you were in temple. To not be there, on a day when even the local public schools were closed, would be unacceptable—no matter how Jew-ish you were. Knowing that, I was pretty sure I also knew what the American Jewish community and its leaders would say about the pope's visit falling on this High Holiday—that the visit might not be about inclusiveness, which was what both the Vatican and the Administration wanted to convey.

Just thinking about the Jewish community's response made me uneasy. My personal and professional worlds were colliding, my past pulling me one way while the pope's visit—which already felt so much larger and more significant than I expected—pulled me another. And for all two of us staffers working in the White House Office of Faith-Based and Neighborhood Partnerships (known alternately as OFBNP, because everything in government has an acronym, or "the faith office" inside the White House, because OFBNP is a terrible acronym), the pope's visit was a BFD. I had to be part of it.

The mission of our office, composed of me and Director Melissa Rogers, was to form partnerships between the federal government and faith-based and community organizations to more effectively serve people in need. Using the Executive Office of the President, we served as the central point for collaboration. We provided information to community organizations, and we listened to the ideas and concerns of their leaders and conveyed them to people throughout government. Day to day, this meant I bounced around from the menial and constant task of scheduling to shaping church-state policy, all the while working with the network of twelve "faith offices" sprinkled throughout federal government—the Centers for Faith-Based and Neighborhood Partnerships (CFBNP). I know—another acronym. While CFBNP offices held a similar mission—to partner with faith and community groups—their work was more focused on a specific topic, depending on which agency housed the office. At the Department of Education, the CFBNP worked on interfaith campus dialogue and programming for college students, and at the Department of Agriculture, CFBNP worked to create opportunities for faith-based and community organizations to provide after-school and summer meals.

One of the benefits of working in OFBNP was that you got to cover an expansive range of policy topics. One day, you'd be working on disaster preparedness and community readiness, and the next, on the international response to the Ebola crisis. Faith community and secular leaders play a role in a wide variety of issues, usually in a supportive role, under the leadership of an expert organization. OFBNP might not have been the first one called to join the meeting, but we'd be there. Yet the visit of His Holiness Pope Francis—well, duh. That was squarely our terrain. OFBNP was not always the popular kid in school, but this was our shining moment. We were seated at the big kids' table in a real way.

The questions to be resolved surrounding the papal visit seemed endless. What worldly issues would the two leaders discuss? What would they each say in their remarks? What policies could we (the Obama Administration) use this visit to advance without overpoliticizing the event? Whom should the pope meet at the White House? What would he care about seeing and hearing? Would Pope Francis appreciate the traditional diplomatic gift exchange or find it frivolous? If they did exchange gifts, what would President Obama present to the pope?

This was no ordinary state visit, and we wanted the events to reflect that. We tossed around some extraordinary or at least unorthodox things the President and the pope could do together. Maybe they could volunteer? Or go to a local public school and read to kids? Several bureaucratic phone calls later—with Vatican officials on a secure line coordinated by our embassy staff across time zones—we bowed to tradition. There would be a formal arrival ceremony on the South Lawn, with a welcome hosted by the President. The ceremony would be accompanied by a long, wordy White House press release entitled "Fact Sheet: Advancing Shared Values for a Better World."

As we narrowed answers to each question surrounding the visit, we identified a short list of topics to discuss—priorities that spoke to the President as well as the pope—from providing refuge for the most vulnerable to promoting sustainable development and ending extreme poverty across the globe. The ultimate goal was to link the government and faith-based organizations to turn shared goals into concrete actions.

Even the early planning stages seemed to generate an unusual level of anticipation for the event. Colleagues across government, everyone from the Visitors Office to Congressional Affairs to the State Department, joined forces to help make sure the visit would live up to the name Pope-apalooza. The Visitors Office was even putting calls out to White House staff for extra volunteers for the arrival ceremony; they needed all hands on deck for such an enormous undertaking. The hype was real.

On every other corner in town, pop-up shops and mobile trucks that sell tchotchkes were suddenly stocked with papal celebratory souvenirs: bobbleheads, mugs, magnets, buttons, T-shirts, holy medallions, and water bottles. I'm not sure how Pope Francis felt about his visit being so monetized. After all, he is a man who is unimpressed by extravagance. But he is also a symbol, the representative of one of the world's largest religions, and people just couldn't help themselves! (At least, I couldn't.)

As with many foreign leaders, there is a long history of popes visiting Washington, DC, and participating in formal state affairs. But this time, we were talking about el papa. Since he assumed the papacy, Pope Francis has galvanized followers across the world—fellow Argentineans and Spanish-speaking Catholics, young Catholics, and secular Catholics. People are drawn to the Church because they like him—they like his uplifting story and his authentic leadership style. What's more, Pope Francis's influence is not limited to Catholics.

I understood that the pope was a public figure before I was assigned this whole papal-visit project, of course. But I did not foresee the celebrity status that *this* pope would have. I'm not sure anyone did. Pope Francis speaks to people of all faiths and no faith. He has proudly taken controversial stands and used unconventional tactics, like when he tweeted his encyclical about climate change, which basically and shockingly said, "Hey, this thing is real" and "Hey, humans, you're a hundred percent part of the problem." (While I admit I had to google the word *encyclical* when I first heard it, I soon got my papal lingo down. I used it to correct—and recorrect—planning documents and to draft statements, becoming an expert in the proper usage of "Holy Father" and "His Holiness" in POTUS memos.)

The magnitude and symbolism of the pope's visit was not lost on me. And I was pretty sure that even my rabbi would approve of my enthusiasm.

★ ★ ★

I went to college at the University of Texas at Austin, where the campus was swarming with thousands of people from different backgrounds with different beliefs (though they were united in their eternal love for the state of Texas). My classmates were eager to learn from the institution—and from one another. It didn't take long during freshman orientation for me to realize that my community was no longer made up of peers whose seventh-grade weekend social calendar was packed with back-to-back bar and bat mitzvah parties. As I immersed myself in this new environment during the heat of the 2008 presidential race, I appreciated how Barack Obama represented an embrace of these differences. I felt as if all people could see themselves in his story and his vision.

I had always been a news junkie, but when I was a freshman, I got my first up-close experience in politics. I volunteered for the Obama campaign. I remember watching campaign events from my dorm room, far from home, listening to a young black man orate as if he were giving a sermon at the pulpit. Obama spoke to the values my parents instilled in me and to the spirit of inclusion and hard work ingrained in me by my upbringing. He also spoke about the value of public service, and I knew that as soon as I graduated, I was going to move to Washington, DC, to answer his call to make the world a better place.

There was only one small matter standing in my way: finding a job. So during my senior year, I applied to the White House Internship Program. I had no expectation that I would get accepted, but somehow I landed an internship with President Obama's Domestic Policy Council. For the next five months, I put my head down and worked. My. Butt. Off. My dedication and positive attitude must have made an impression, because a year and a half later, post-internship, when I was plugging away at a Jewish nonprofit organization focused on anti-poverty and civil rights work, I got a call from a blocked number at the White House asking me if

I'd be interested in coming back on as staff. I couldn't say yes fast enough.

★ ★ ★

So there I was, the only Jewish staffer in OFBNP working on the papal visit that was set to take place on Yom Kippur. Much of my energy during the previous weeks and months had been focused on this one day. The work, to be sure, was incredibly rewarding. It also tested me in unexpected ways.

Such was the case on an August day when there was a papal-visit coordinating meeting. This meeting, held in the Diplomatic Reception Room, brought together some of the most important voices in the federal government, including representatives from the State Department and Secret Service. That morning, my boss oh-so-casually let me know that she wouldn't be able to lead this important meeting. She had a papal-planning conflict, likely discussing the same exact things with a different audience in another meeting that outranked this one. She was handing the meeting responsibilities over to me. I froze.

I stared at my computer, rereading the emailed agenda with *my name on it*, imposter syndrome intensifying with each passing second.

Taking in my stonelike posture, Ashley Allison, my office mate and older, wiser friend, intervened. "T! You're fine. You know this stuff cold." I looked at her with trepidation, but she was having none of it. She grabbed the binder on my desk, the one I'd need for the meeting, shoved it under my arm, and pushed me out the door. "Get your ass upstairs."

I marched up a flight of marble stairs and click-clicked down the hallway in my kitten heels. *Smile,* I told myself. I faked a smile. If there had been time to stand in a bathroom stall in a power pose, the proud Superman stance with hands on hips, I would have done it. (I've used that technique before, and I swear it worked.) Instead, I told myself again, *Just smile.*

Inside the room was a table surrounded by unfamiliar faces, all in suits or uniforms. They all looked pretty important. I felt like everyone knew one another and had worked together on past state visits. If I pretended I was part of this cohort, would they believe it? I had never before been in a meeting with Secret Service agents present.

The armchair felt big. I was aware of my posture, of sitting straighter than usual. For a time, I listened closely, taking in complicated presentations about logistics and security. When it was my turn to present, I locked eyes with a senior White House Communications staffer. She kindly smiled at me, and I launched in.

I presented the OFBNP's plan, detailing the work that brought together public groups and private individuals. I talked about the announcements we would make through the White House Fact Sheet and how these actions and new partnerships centering on poverty, the environment, and refugee support would reinforce the values shared by the President and the pope. As I talked, whatever anxieties had overwhelmed me just a few minutes earlier seemed to disappear. These issues mattered to me. They mattered a lot.

By the time the meeting ended, my smile came easily. I had nailed it. I gathered my binder and marched back toward the office. Ashley was standing in the hallway, talking with a colleague. When I walked past, she held out her hand for a quick fist bump, and I casually pounded it. Feeling proud, I hurried back to my office to focus on what I could only assume was an exploding in-box of unread emails.

★ ★ ★

On the eve of the pope's visit, that August day in the Diplomatic Reception Room seemed like so long ago. I surveyed my desk, where my friend Molly had left a "survival kit": energy bars, water, Advil, and, peeking out of the bag, a paper cutout of the pope glued to a Popsicle stick. I nodded to mini Pope Francis, turned off the lights, and said, "Good night, Your Holiness."

I popped up when the alarm went off at 4:30 and shut off the other three. I quickly fluffed the couch pillows and threw on my outfit—a hot-pink blazer with pockets, a black shift dress, and flats. I had an understanding with my family that at big public events where there were lots of cameras, I would wear bright colors so they could try to spot me on TV. Thus the pink blazer. The pockets were also a deliberate choice. I always used them on big event days for my phones—both personal and work—pens, papers, or any items thrown at me.

Sleepy-eyed staffers huddled in the hallway. Even though we had spent the night at the office, we had to exit the White House grounds and reenter at another security checkpoint on the opposite side of campus, as if we were just arriving for work. We walked out of the brightly lit building hallways and into the darkness outside. We zigzagged through the security barriers to get off campus on the west side and then zigzagged through more security barriers on the east side to use the proper entrance. The sun was just rising when I arrived at my assigned station outside the East Wing.

It was chilly and dewy on the lawn, but I could tell it was going to be a beautiful sunny morning. Guests flooded the South Lawn; I felt a wave of energy and excitement. There was a VIP entrance off the East Wing and through the Jacqueline Kennedy Garden. My mission was to escort VIPs to their assigned seats and make sure they were settled (and happy!) in time for the ceremony start time at 9:15 a.m. Everything at the White House—daily schedules, meetings, and especially events—was timed to the minute.

I had been given a list of names. Some people I already knew because I had worked with them, like the prominent national Catholic and Christian leaders, as well as Sikh, Hindu, and Buddhist leaders. Others were true celebrities. I escorted Robert F. Kennedy Jr. and Cheryl Hines to their seats. To be honest, I recognized Cheryl first. I had created my own personal Facebook binder to try to memorize the faces and names of those I didn't know. Of course, I failed to actually study my guide, but I hoped that the act of creating it had ingrained *something* on my memory. As the morning unfolded, the folks on my list happily stayed put in their seats and socialized in a pleasant fashion. The members of Congress, on the other hand, were a bit unruly. *Surprise, surprise.* They milled about on the lawn, schmoozing and loudly joking with one another.

In case of an emergency, the Visitors Office had arranged for a water and snack station on the lawn. I was near it when suddenly, Senator Bernie Sanders was standing next to me. With his arms crossed over his body, a bit aloof, he watched the hustle on the lawn. This was in the middle of the 2016 election, and Bernie's presidential run was picking up steam across the country. A colleague came by, nodded toward the White House, and joked, "Getting used to the view, eh, Bernie?" Senator Sanders brushed it off as he noshed on two granola bars and then stood there for a while picking them out of his teeth. Thank God we had that fuel for "emergency purposes."

I pinched my colleague from the Office of Legislative Affairs and signaled toward Senator Sanders. I'd let her handle that one. My stakeholders were behaving properly!

At 9:10 a.m., the ceremony was just about to begin. I shuffled to the left side of the lawn and saw some empty seats. I filled in the gap by taking an empty chair and nodded to some colleagues to do the same. It wasn't until I looked up that I realized I was not more than twenty feet from the stage. I would be able to see *everything*—President Obama and the Holy Father, every gesture, every interaction.

The military band broke into a drumroll, and the doors to the White House swung open. The voice of god—that's what we called the announcer's booming voice in the POTUS memo—came over the loudspeaker and introduced the President and Mrs. Obama. They stepped onto the red carpet to wait for the pope's car to arrive. As the crowd roared, the small black Fiat pulled up. The first thing I spotted was the top of the white zucchetto (It's like a yarmulke! Shout-out to all my peeps at temple who observed Yom Kippur instead of YOPO-ing) as he got out of the car.

The Obamas and the Holy Father shook hands. As if from nowhere, a small man in a black robe appeared and whispered in the pope's ear. It was Monsignor Mark Miles, who served as a translator—and apparently something of a magician. *Where did he come from?* I wondered. Had he also gotten out of that black Fiat that just rolled up?

As the President and the Holy Father stepped onto the small stage, the crowd of eleven thousand erupted again. In front of the stage, there was a vast roped-off swath of grass with a row of risers at the base for the lucky few seated guests. There were a few hundred chairs near the stage for even luckier guests—the VIPs. Behind the risers, thousands of guests stood on the lawn. There were large projection screens positioned farther down the lawn so people could watch the ceremony.

The military band played the national anthems of the Holy See and the United States as the pope and President Obama, in their floor-length white robe and black suit respectively, stood tall and proud. The pope took his seat onstage when the President walked to the podium. The President was to speak first, followed by the pope. The President began by welcoming the Holy Father to the White House and to the United States. He addressed the pope directly and also spoke to the American people and the crowd. President Obama acknowledged how excited all Americans, from every background and every faith, were to welcome the Holy Father to the United States and how his leadership of the Church—and his unique qualities as a person—resonated in this country.

The President referenced his time as a community organizer working with the Catholic Church on the South Side of Chicago. He spoke of the pope's humility and embrace of simplicity, and then talked about shared values and missions of the Catholic Church and the United States, like religious freedom and welcoming the stranger. He specifically thanked the Holy Father for his help in reopening relations with Cuba earlier in the year and joined the pope in his call for global leaders to address climate change and protect our common home.

At the end of his speech, the President spoke about the Holy Father's inspiring moral example. These words, uttered by one of my heroes quoting a hero to the world, brought home the presence and power of these men and this occasion. President Obama said:

> You . . . give us confidence that we can come together in humility and service, and pursue a world that is more loving, more just, and more free. Here at home and around the world, may our generation heed your call to "never remain on the sidelines of this march of living hope."

The President had gone through a few rounds of edits on his speech, which was pretty normal. It was hard to encapsulate such a meaningful experience in just ten minutes, but as usual, with all credit to the President and his speechwriting team, POTUS pulled it off.

The two leaders shook hands again and smiled politely. The pope is quite the polyglot, but I worried about a language barrier. English is not his strength. As he walked to the podium to take his turn speaking, again Monsignor Mark Miles discreetly appeared onstage to place the speech on the lectern and offer His Holiness a sip of water. Pope Francis dug into his pocket to pull out his reading glasses. I was unnecessarily nervous. He scanned the audience, and as he slowly pronounced, "Good morning," I let out a sigh of joy and relief.

Each of his words was slow, deliberate, and graceful. He thanked the Obamas and expressed his excitement to be in the United States. He spoke broadly about the same themes the President had touched on—see, we had done *some* coordinating with the Vatican in advance—and spoke of his dream for America and the world to build a society that is tolerant, inclusive, and just and protects the vulnerable.

When he concluded, the two men shook hands (again!), and the pope took his seat while we listened to the St. Augustine Gospel Choir from Washington, DC, perform. As the President and the pope walked back down the red carpet toward the White House, Mrs. Obama joined them. Side by side, the Obamas towered over Pope Francis. Someone in the crowd bellowed in a deep voice, "We love you, Pope Francis," and again the crowd erupted in cheers. His back was to the crowd, but I could see the Holy Father grin slightly.

Everyone remained standing and clapping. Thirty seconds later, the pope appeared on the balcony, still sandwiched between POTUS and FLOTUS. They waved to the masses and disappeared back into the house, leaving me thinking about how glad I was to be there, to have just witnessed history from twenty feet away.

After the ceremony, the crowds shuffled off the lawn. Inside the White House, Pope Francis and President Obama did formal introductions and exchanged gifts. President Obama gave the pope two things: a custom sculpture of a dove made from a piece of the original Statue of Liberty and wood from the White House lawn, and a 206-year-old key from the home of Elizabeth Ann Seton, the first native-born American to be declared a saint, who had been canonized forty years earlier. The dove is the international symbol of peace and represents the Holy Spirit in Christianity. In return, Pope Francis presented a bronze bas-relief plaque commemorating the 2015 World Meeting of Families, happening later that week in Philadelphia.

Toward the end of a short tour, leaving his staff behind to watch, President Obama and Pope Francis stepped onto the colonnade between the White House residence and the West Wing and the Oval Office. This is the famous forty-five-second walk between the office and home that is in tons of photographs and videos—the one the President took daily to go to work and to return home for dinner with Mrs. Obama and their kids.

I knew this was a ready-made photo opportunity—the two of them strolling next to the Rose Garden, which was in bloom. President Obama signaled a few points of interest while Pope Francis smiled and nodded along. And just as I was wondering if he understood any of what the President was saying, Monsignor Mark Miles popped up, as if conjured from air, and whispered in the pope's ear.

Suddenly, the morning was over. I stood on the front lawn, peering at the West Wing driveway, where a procession of black SUVs and police cars was lined up. The white Popemobile stuck out like a sore thumb. It was a modified Jeep, open on either side to afford the expectant crowds unrestricted views. Pope Francis climbed in, ready to greet the many thousands of adoring fans who had traveled to Washington, DC, from far and wide to see him.

The adrenaline of the morning had propelled me through, but now I needed coffee. Badly. The motorcade began rolling, and the Popemobile inched down the driveway and out the gates to the street. I let out a sigh of relief and waved goodbye to His Holiness Pope Francis.

YOPO.

VIVIAN P. GRAUBARD

Title: Confidential Assistant and Advisor to the United States
Chief Technology Officer
Office: Office of Science and Technology Policy
Age: 24
Date: December 6, 2013

I've been unable to sleep only twice in my life. The first time was in January 2010. I was a junior in college and a communications fellow at Polaris Project, an organization dedicated to combating modern-day slavery. A few weeks into the program, the fellows were instructed by their managers to meet at the office at midnight. We were told that we'd be going on a night tour of human trafficking hot spots. To keep myself awake past my usual bedtime, I binged a few episodes of *The Office* and then, around eleven p.m., put on my heaviest coat and a pair of boots and headed into the office, unsure where the night would take us.

After a quick huddle with two staff members, who explained that they'd be taking us to locations where traffickers were known to be operating, we boarded a van with blacked-out windows and our ride-along began. I knew that human trafficking was prevalent, but I was surprised to learn just how close to home it really was: The massage parlor next to a bar I routinely visited on nights out with friends. The kitchen of a restaurant in my neighborhood. An adult club I passed every morning on my daily run. These places were hidden in plain sight. And once they were exposed to me, the problem was impossible to ignore.

That night ended at the Lincoln Memorial. The fresh snow blended perfectly with the white marble as we sat along the steps and looked out at the reflecting pool, contemplating a future truly free from slavery. While the history of forced labor in the United States differs greatly from the contemporary experience of human trafficking, both represent a form of slavery. Concluding the night here felt appropriate. The Lincoln Memorial, illuminated by the predawn light, reminded me of how far we have come and how far we have left to go. Above all, I felt a sense of determination and hope for what the new day could bring.

When I got back to my apartment around six a.m., McDonald's breakfast sandwich in hand, I told myself that I'd try to get some sleep before my class later that afternoon. Every time I closed my eyes, though, all I could think about was the abuse and terror happening all around me. I was existing in a frozen place between light and dark, good and bad, understanding and ignorance.

It would be years before I'd endure another sleepless night.

The December after the ride-along, I graduated from college, overwhelmed with anxiety about where my life was heading. Everywhere I looked, it felt like my peers had figured out their next steps, were moving on, or were somehow sure of their lives in a way I was not. Then, out of the blue, someone from the Latin American Student Organization sent an email about a volunteer opportunity at the White House. With no plans, apart from traveling to China to visit my younger brother, I decided to submit an application to volunteer a few hours each week in the Office of Presidential Correspondence, aka the President's mailroom.

The office soon got in touch with me and scheduled an orientation for later that week. The other volunteers and I would read, sort, and tag the thousands of letters, emails, and faxes that arrive for the President every day. When I showed up on the first day, however, the volunteer coordinator, Matt Schaub, glanced at my résumé and said, "Oh, you have a tech background?"

I nodded. "I have a double major in international business and IT."

Matt had a larger-than-life personality with a smile twice the size. "Great!" he said, flashing me one of his signature smiles. He explained that the office had a few tech projects and could use some additional support. He asked if I wanted to pitch in on those.

I didn't know then what was in store for me, and didn't fully recognize the huge opportunity that had just presented itself, but eager to help, I enthusiastically agreed.

Matt then introduced me to Martin Cuellar, who would soon become my first boss.

For months, I worked full-time as an unpaid volunteer to help the Office of Presidential Correspondence scope out a new digital White House Comment Line. The existing system was largely paper-based, and involved volunteers like me taking phone calls throughout the day from people leaving comments on a broad range of issues—from expressing support for immigration reform to relating frustrations with the economy. These volunteers would tally how many people called each day and note support or opposition on hundreds of issues. At the end of the day, interns would manually enter the tallies into an Excel spreadsheet, which was then used to generate reports for the West Wing. For the President, this was the clearest, most unobscured snapshot of how people were feeling across the country—and around the globe. Anybody could call, and someone would always answer. And save the threatening or disrespectful calls, someone was always there to listen.

Sometimes, when the comment line was short-staffed, they'd pull volunteers from other departments to help with the influx of calls. I can still remember a few of my favorites—like a phone call from a fellow Cuban American expressing support for the President. We bonded over being from Miami, and when I told her that my father was from Colombia and my mother was Puerto Rican and Cuban, we promptly switched to speaking Spanish. She told me how proud she was to hear that a fellow Latina was at the White House! Then there were the phone calls that brought me to tears, like the ones from Gold Star parents whose children lost their lives serving in the military, or from parents who had been unable to afford health insurance for their children, who lost their battles with cancer. Because there were so many people calling, we were told to keep calls to a few minutes—less than two if possible. But there were always calls that were just too difficult to end.

I was coming back from grabbing coffee at Swings (a coffee shop frequented by White House staff) when Martin told me that the Deputy Director for Technology, Michael Hornsby, was transitioning to a new office and my colleague, Jason Smith, was being promoted to his role. This left Jason's position open, and if I was interested, I could apply for it.

And so June 6, 2011, became my first official day as a White House staffer.

Our team was responsible for improving the technical tools used to track and respond to messages sent to the President. And I got to spend a lot of time on my favorite project: figuring out how to respond to foreign-language correspondence. Previously, letters in a language other than English were put aside until there were enough of them to send to the State Department for translation. Even then, they were only translated to ensure that the writer hadn't made any threats. If you wrote to the President in English, you were sure to get a response from the Office of Presidential Correspondence. But if you wrote to the President in any other language, you simply wouldn't hear back.

This seemed unfair to me. For starters, writing in a language other than English does not preclude you from being a citizen. Many of the Spanish letters I read were from citizens. They too were Americans. And they deserved a response.

Martin encouraged me to assemble a group of volunteers who spoke foreign languages and spend a few hours with them each week building a new rules engine in our system that would identify the subject of a writer's letter. We started with Spanish, because it was my first language, but from there, it was easy to move on to similar languages, like Italian and Portuguese.

Soon after we processed the first foreign-language letters, Jason alerted me that he'd also be joining another team at the White House. With his departure, I thought I'd be the obvious candidate for his role as Deputy Director for Technology.

I was wrong.

Instead, the role went to a colleague from another department. And while I liked him well enough as a person, I learned that I'd be left to carry Jason's workload plus my own while training my new boss at his job. It's hard to know whether age or experience factored into the decision to promote him over me, but as I sat in the director's office saying I understood the decision, I was actually screaming internally.

I went home that night momentarily defeated, but ultimately I decided that I'd put my best foot forward at work and continue to do the job the next day.

A few weeks after getting passed over for the promotion, I attended an event at South Court Auditorium—where most large White House events take place—hosted by the Office of Science and Technology Policy. Dr. John Holdren, President Obama's advisor on all things science, was speaking to a group of high school students about the importance of STEM education. Specifically, he spoke of how critical it was for young women and students of color to take an interest in and pursue careers in the sciences. He acknowledged that it might be a lonely path, that often, scientists and engineers didn't look like those of us in the audience. I already knew they rarely looked like me.

When the talk was over, I stayed behind to say hello to Lauren Andersen, the woman who had organized and invited me to the event. Lauren was an advisor at the Office of Science and Technology Policy. I recall feeling intimidated by her. She was smart, ambitious, and charismatic. A few minutes into the conversation, she asked me how I liked working at the Office of Presidential Correspondence.

Normally, I might have said something that wouldn't require much follow-up, like *It's fine!* But with the memory of being passed over for a promotion fresh in my mind, I decided to be bold and honest. I surprised even myself, though, when the words tumbled out: "I've enjoyed my time there, but recently I've been thinking about next steps."

"Hmmm . . . ," she said, and I immediately regretted my words. Had I been too candid, too soon? But then she told me that the new Chief Technology Officer, Todd Park, was looking for a Confidential Assistant. "If you're interested, I'll pass your name along to PPO," she said. PPO was the Office of Presidential Personnel, which was responsible for hiring and recruiting to fill political appointee slots across government. I was thrilled.

The interview would happen in three parts: First, an interview with a PPO staffer. Next, a panel interview with the Chief of Staff of the Office of Science and Technology Policy and two advisors from the Office of the Chief Technology Officer. And finally, an interview with the CTO himself, Todd Park.

I left the first interview feeling confident—until a friend who worked at PPO told me that I shouldn't get my hopes up because there were other candidates with more experience who had "worked in tech" before. I did my best not to let his words get to me, and fortunately was able to distract myself with an upcoming trip. The next day, I was leaving for Denver to visit my best friend and college roommate, Jessica Reinhardt. I just had to get through one more day of work and then I'd head to the airport that evening.

As I was leaving for the airport, I found out that I had made it to the final round—I would meet Todd Park—and that the interview would happen after Todd returned from traveling the following week. *Good timing,* I thought. *Maybe I'll run into him at the airport,* I jokingly imagined as I pulled my carry-on out the door.

I had taken my seat on the plane and was waiting for boarding to finish when I noticed a familiar person walking down the aisle. Though I'd never actually met him, I knew his face from obsessive googling (*for interview prep!*). It was definitely him. My—maybe—soon-to-be boss!

He, of course, had no idea who I was.

I knew I had to introduce myself. As the plane took off, I contemplated how this interaction might take place. Was I supposed to just walk up to him, on a plane, and say hello?

Well, yeah, obviously.

I got up from my seat and started walking toward him, when I decided that I just couldn't do it. What if he thought I was stalking him? So I continued up the aisle until I reached the bathroom and there was nowhere else to go. I went in, stood there for a few minutes and gave myself a pep talk, then walked back out.

I would pass him again on the way down the aisle, so if I planned on saying hello, now was the time. I walked forward, when suddenly, my feet froze at seat 8C. He was on his Black-Berry, rapidly typing. I thought it would be rude to interrupt, but I'd also been standing there for a few seconds, and it was going to be weird if I didn't say something or move along.

So I tapped him on the shoulder. He looked up from his phone and said, in a kind voice, "Yes?"

"Mr. Park," I responded, "you don't know me. My name is Vivian Graubard, and next week I'm going to interview to be your Confidential Assistant."

Todd took a moment before saying, "Oh, and . . . what are you doing on this flight?"

To my surprise, his tone was that of genuine curiosity and not concern. I assured him that I hadn't tracked his flight and followed him here, but that I was going to visit a friend and our paths crossing was just one big, wonderful coincidence.

When the flight landed, we spoke for a few minutes on the train to the baggage claim before parting ways. He told me briefly about his goals in his new role as Chief Technology Officer and about his previous work at the Department of Health and Human Services.

The next day I called Michael, the Deputy Director I had worked with at the Office of Presidential Correspondence, to tell him about my chance encounter with Todd. "Some things are just meant to be," he said.

When it came time for my interview with Todd, I met him at his office in the Eisenhower Executive Office Building, where most of the White House staff works. We exchanged pleasantries about our trips before diving into the interview.

From my résumé, he saw that I had spent time in India. He too had worked there on a venture he created called Healthpoint Services, which brought affordable clean water, drugs, diagnostics, and telehealth services to rural villages.

He asked about my passions, and instead I gave an answer related to the role I was applying for as his Confidential Assistant. But he pressed me. He didn't want to know why I wanted to be his assistant, scheduling his meetings and putting together his daily briefing book. He wanted to know what work I loved to do. That was when I told him about the issue closest to my heart: combating modern-day slavery. That was the work that had taken me to India, and one day, I hoped I would find a way to merge my background in technology with my passion for anti-trafficking efforts.

A few days later, my phone rang. On the other end, telling me that I'd gotten the job, wasn't a PPO staffer. It was Todd himself. I was at happy hour and I ran out of the bar when I realized it was him. We spoke for a few minutes and then I went back in, eager to tell my friends the good news. With a few minutes left before the drink specials ended, we all raised a toast to my next adventure.

I started in May 2012, right around my twenty-third birthday. I arrived at the office the first day to find balloons and cards signed by other staff at OSTP—including Lauren! It was a warm welcome to the team, and as the job began to require more and more of my time, the office quite literally became a home to me. I left shoes and clothes at my desk and showered in the gym there most mornings after long runs into work.

Todd had a busy schedule, jam-packed with commitments and speaking events and requests for meetings from people eager to pitch him ideas. And the requests never stopped coming. I'd get to the office by seven-thirty a.m. to make sure everything was set for the day, and I'd usually stay until eight p.m. I'd get home, make dinner (sometimes), and continue responding to emails into the early-morning hours.

But Todd also worked long hours, and I wanted to prove that I could keep up. We instantly clicked, and I came to appreciate that despite being the boss, he didn't presume to know everything. He listened in every meeting and diligently took notes. He never interrupted, taking a moment to pause before asking questions to make sure he understood the information he was being briefed on.

This was something I noticed many of President Obama's senior advisors had in common. They were not arrogant; they respected the advice of experts, and they took in as much information as possible, fully digesting it before coming to a decision.

Todd told me early on that I was welcome to attend any meetings or events with him that sounded interesting. I appreciated that just as he was eager to learn, he was generous in offering me the same opportunities. On any given day, I'd attend meetings that spanned topics from spectrum and broadband access to transforming health care through data. I was learning so much, so quickly.

But I was still his assistant. And there were many people in the office who wanted to make sure I knew my place. Todd was never one of them, and I was able to persevere because, in him, I'd found a mentor, a champion, and an advocate. Over time, I was promoted to the role of Advisor and then Senior Advisor to the U.S. Chief Technology Officer.

In July of 2012, Todd was invited to an event at Microsoft in Redmond, Washington. The Microsoft Research Faculty Summit brought together academic researchers, engineers, and educators to discuss social challenges that could potentially be solved through the sciences. At the summit, a researcher named danah boyd was leading a discussion on how technology was changing the way human trafficking was happening. Posting advertisements for women and children online, she said, was just one of the ways traffickers were using the internet to their benefit. What was unclear was how, and if, we could use technology to our advantage to address the problem.

This event inspired my first policy portfolio, or area of expertise, at the White House: using technology and data to combat human trafficking.

★ ★ ★

As a Policy Advisor to the Chief Technology Officer, I collaborated with other offices that were also identifying ways to combat human trafficking. One afternoon I was invited to a meeting in the First Lady's Office in the East Wing. Tina Tchen, the Executive Director of the Council on Women and Girls, had convened multiple offices to discuss how anti-trafficking efforts were progressing. I was introduced to two women who would become my coconspirators in using technology to fight crime: Lynn Overmann and Hallie Schneir.

The three of us organized events and meetings that brought together the tech sector and anti-trafficking stakeholders to identify solutions for combating modern-day slavery. We also worked to connect survivors with much-needed services, like housing, health care, and legal support. At the annual TED conference in Long Beach, California, I spoke about human trafficking with Nancy Lublin, the founder of DoSomething.org, in front of thousands of people. Bill Gates and other high-profile TED attendees were in the front row as I explained that this was not just an international issue but was also happening in the United States— and likely in their very own city.

We worked with a sense of urgency. The West Wing was prioritizing the anti-trafficking policy agenda, and we had to push as much work through as possible while we still had their attention. In September 2012, President Obama dedicated his entire speech at the Clinton Global Initiative to talking about human trafficking and, above all, our collective need to bring it to an end. This was a huge opportunity for the entire field because every September, all of the world's leaders descend on New York for the United Nations General Assembly, and the Clinton Global Initiative was strategically hosted at around the same time.

In preparation for the event, the President's speechwriters reached out to policy staff, as was their usual process, seeking substantive contributions to his remarks. Dozens of staffers worked long hours in the weeks leading up to the event to provide content for the speech. Every word was carefully curated, every emphasis thoughtfully placed. No detail was too small. Every fact was to be checked; every person's name was to be vetted.

I watched the speech come together, from a document with dozens of authors and hundreds of comments to the beautiful, moving, and hard-hitting overture the public heard. As I'd come to expect from President Obama's public remarks, what little room there was for spontaneity he filled gracefully and with precise attention to the facts of the matter. It was hard not to call my parents and tell them about the process leading up to the big day, but we weren't allowed to share information on speeches beforehand. On the morning of the event, I called to tell them that they could watch the President's speech live on the White House website and instructed them to listen for the following words:

> . . . we're turning the tables on the traffickers. Just as they are now using technology and the Internet to exploit their victims, we're going to harness technology

to stop them. We're encouraging tech companies and advocates and law enforcement—and we're also challenging college students—to develop tools that our young people can use to stay safe online and on their smartphones.

I don't think I'll ever forget the feeling of hearing President Obama talk about work that I'd done, and that I cared so deeply about, on a global stage.

The President's speech was a loud, public renewal of the United States' commitment to end modern-day slavery. And every agency, every office, could feel the increased pressure to deliver on our goals. As part of its annual commitments, the State Department had planned a series of international TechCamps, weeklong workshops where technologists were paired with advocates to identify solutions to global challenges. Their second anti-trafficking TechCamp would take place in Tlaxcala, Mexico, and I was asked to speak on the opening night.

A few days before the trip, I had gone to the New Executive Office Building across the street from the White House to complete a passport application and have my picture taken so that I could travel on behalf of the U.S. government (you couldn't use your personal passport). I filled out the forms in a hurry between meetings: *Gender: Female; Age: 24; Place of Birth: Pembroke Pines, Florida.* As I stood for my photo, I thought, "Maybe I should have done my hair today," shrugged, and quickly smiled before the flash. A few minutes later, I was holding it in my hands. A fresh new passport that read "OFFICIAL" on the front.

"Finally," I thought, "I've made it." All my work and volunteer hours at the Office of Presidential Correspondence, my time as Todd's assistant, the many long nights at the office had brought me to this point—where I was capable of representing the White House abroad.

★ ★ ★

On the flight to Mexico, I reviewed fact sheets and read policy papers, recommitting to memory everything I knew about human trafficking and the work we had been doing to combat it. I also read up on the region we would be visiting. Tlaxcala was a small state known for its talaveras (clay pottery) but had become a hotbed for international human trafficking in recent years. Here, young boys aspired to become pimps, and girls were being courted and lured into sex trafficking at alarming rates. Tenancingo, a town in Tlaxcala with a population of ten thousand, estimated that roughly 10 percent of their community was involved in trafficking—and that the industry there had generated over $1 billion in revenue.

Tenancingo was a town in crisis. Over the course of two days, technologists were paired with advocates to brainstorm ways that technology could be used to support anti-trafficking efforts. From secure online storage with Google Drive and Dropbox to social media training, we planned to introduce simple tech tools with the potential to have a massive impact on their organizational efficiency. This was exciting not only due to the impact these tools would have on the community in Tlaxcala but also as a way to show how technology, even when it's as simple as shared documents, can be a powerful force for good. I had spent a lot of time at the White House convincing senior advisors and key stakeholders that technology is a critical consideration for all our projects, and now I'd be part of proving my case on the ground.

As a young Latina, I also felt proud to be representing the United States in Latin America. Often, I felt disconnected from my Latin roots, but here I felt right at home. The sun and the sound of people speaking Spanish everywhere reminded me of summers in Colombia and Puerto Rico. I felt a certain kinship to the other attendees, the kind of bond that comes from having a shared language and a shared culture and from wanting desperately to see your community thrive.

The first night in Mexico, I was asked to give remarks following the U.S. Ambassador to Mexico, Anthony Wayne. I had spent a lot of time over the past two weeks preparing for this moment. Though I spoke Spanish fluently, I mostly used it at home and in conversation with family and friends. I was worried that my accent wasn't good enough, or that I'd stumble when using professional terms that I didn't use in my everyday Spanish. My heart was racing, but I managed to get through the speech quickly and without any major mistakes. The night ended on a high note, and I was eager for what the next day would bring.

Though it wasn't what I was expecting, the second day did bring unexpected excitement: during lunch, I got an email from the editors at *Time* magazine. They told me that I had been nominated for their "30 Under 30" list and they needed my bio and a headshot. They emphasized that a final decision had not been made and that this did not mean I was definitely on the list, but I couldn't help feeling thrilled and proud.

But any excitement about the *Time* nomination was quickly dulled when I faced the stark reality in Mexico. That evening, and over the next two days, attendees shared heartbreaking stories about the tragedies caused by human trafficking. One woman, who was also Colombian, told us about how she'd been tricked into taking a job that was falsely advertised for nannying services abroad. Instead, her passport was confiscated, and she was taken to a hotel room in a city she didn't know, where she didn't speak the language, and sexually exploited for profit. It would be months before she was rescued and able to go home to her family.

There were dozens more stories just like hers. I cared about combating human trafficking because I felt it was an injustice that needed to end. Other attendees cared about it because their lives had been forever changed as a result of it.

I wasn't prepared for the most tragic story of all, though. On the third day of TechCamp, I was walking through the hotel in between sessions when another attendee asked me if I had a moment to chat privately. She suggested we speak in her room, which was nearby.

Slowly, painfully, she proceeded to tell me about her daughter. She guessed that I was around the same age her daughter would be now—early twenties. Every day, her daughter had come directly home from school to do her homework and help around the house. One day, she simply didn't return. At first, she thought her daughter might be with friends. And though that was out of character, she tried to put her mind at ease. But when night fell, she knew something was wrong. The mother immediately called the police to report her daughter missing. They lived in a small, rural town. The kind of town where everyone knew each other.

The police officer who answered the phone told her that he had often seen her daughter hanging around older men. She knew this to be false. He said that she had a new boyfriend, and that she was probably with him. Again, false. He told her that her daughter had likely run away, like so many other girls had. All false. She pleaded with the police officer to help her look, but he said that her daughter would probably be home soon and hung up.

Days turned into weeks turned into months—and there was no sign of her daughter. She'd begun to hear whispers around town that other young girls had also gone missing and were unaccounted for. Surely they hadn't all run off with boyfriends. So she began to gather information. The date and time when each girl had last been seen, where they were, who they might have been with. Increasingly, members of the community were becoming convinced that the young girls in their town were being sold into sex trafficking, and this woman was leading the charge to uncover the truth.

She was walking through the town square one afternoon when a large man approached her and hit her on the head. As she fell to the ground, she heard him saying something. She couldn't be sure what the exact words were, but the message was clear: *Stop looking or else.*

Still, she remained committed to finding her daughter. She had built a coalition of mothers and parents whose children had inexplicably gone missing, and despite threats, despite her house being set on fire, and despite menacing phone calls, she didn't stop.

I tried to fight the tears and I wondered why she was telling me this story at all. Was it because I reminded her of her daughter? Because I worked at the White House and she thought I could do something about it?

But then she gave me a hug and it became clear. She wanted me to listen, to understand what people very far away from the White House were experiencing. At best, her story could inform our approach to policy. In that moment, though, we were just two people. She was a mother, and I was a daughter.

I thanked her for sharing her story with me, and we made our way back to the event, each caught up in our own world of memories and sadness, and with a drive to end the system that had taken her daughter away.

That night, the same sleeplessness I had experienced after the ride-along in DC washed over me. I replayed the mother's story over and over in my mind. I wondered how she could possibly summon the courage to wake up every day and continue to live her life without her daughter. I thought of my own parents, my mom, and how it had been a few days since we had spoken. I was consumed by these thoughts until, finally, the sun rose and it was time to go to breakfast.

I made my way down to the hotel restaurant, sat with attendees from the TechCamp with whom I had become fast friends, and talked about how we felt the event had gone. It was between my second and third cafés con leche that a notification lit up the screen of my BlackBerry. It was an email from a writer at *Time,* and it simply read "Hey, Vivian—congrats" with a smiley face followed by a link. I let out a high-pitched shriek when I saw that the link led to my picture under the headline "These Are the 30 People Under 30 Changing the World."

I was being recognized for my efforts to combat trafficking with technology. I went back to my hotel room after breakfast, feeling both exuberant and exhausted, to finish packing my bags before heading downstairs to take the bus back to Mexico City.

As those of us who were traveling to the airport said goodbye to the rest of the attendees in the hotel lobby, the mother from the day before waved me over. *"¿Como amaneciste?"* she asked. It was a way of asking how I'd woken up and how I'd slept the night before. I lied and told her I slept well, and asked how she was doing. Perhaps also lying, or perhaps because she was braver than I was, she told me that she had slept well and that she was having a great morning. She then pulled something from her bag. It was a talavera cross, and it was for me. The cross was delicate and intricate, and inscribed on the back was "Tlaxcala, Mexico."

She told me that she wanted me to have something beautiful to remember Mexico by. She understood that the past few days had been spent talking about the ugliest parts of what was happening in their region, but there were beautiful things to be found here too. This cross was one of them. I couldn't believe that this woman, who was grieving her missing daughter, could still find it within herself to give me such an incredible gift. She wasn't just giving me a cross; she was giving me hope.

I spent the whole bus ride to the airport thinking about that woman. In a few hours, I would land at Dulles Airport in Virginia, thousands of miles away from Tlaxcala. That mother's daughter could be just as far away, but she still fought every day to find her. That alone could give me hope, couldn't it?

★ ★ ★

Back in the United States, I looked out the window of the cab, comparing the scenery to Mexico's. There, it was warm and sunny. In DC, it was cold and dark. I called my parents to let them know I had landed safely and to finally share the *Time* news with them. Conversations with my mom always started the same way:

"Hola, mi vida." (Literally "Hello, my life" but closer to "my world, my love.")

"¿Hola, mami, como estas?" ("Hi, Mom, how are you?")

"¿Bien, mi amorcito, y tu?" ("Good, my love, and you?")

But when I opened my mouth to speak, making the *Time* list suddenly didn't seem that important. Instead, I recounted highlights of my trip and shared some of the stories I'd heard. (I couldn't bring myself to tell her about the mother and her missing daughter, though—it would upset her too much.) At the end of the call, I finally mentioned the list. I had, of course, already shared the news on Facebook at the airport, so she had seen it, but she was waiting for me to bring it up. My parents were overjoyed and told me how proud they were. *"Te quiero mucho."* ("I love you so much.")

I hung up the phone and pushed open the door to my apartment, but I didn't unpack. Mainly because I'm a self-admitted disaster, but also because sometimes, taking the space to just pause and breathe is the best thing you can do. Before I crawled into my bed, however, I pulled the cross from my bag and tucked it into my closet, in the special place I have between my cozy sweaters where I keep all my most important things. It joined a T-shirt that belonged to my grandfather, Papa, and the ceramic paw print of my dog, Nena, who had passed away a few months before.

Snuggled in my pajamas, I grabbed my BlackBerry and began to check all the emails I had missed while in Mexico. It felt so strange, immersing myself in the everyday normalcy when I felt so changed. I decided after a few minutes to put my phone away and try to remember what I had seen, heard, and learned the past few days.

I thought about the woman who had been trafficked and now bravely shares her story, despite the nonbelievers, with the hope of preventing someone else from suffering a similar fate. The mother with the missing daughter, who lives her life every day with unimaginable grace and determination in the face of so much pain, and who still finds the strength to give to others. I thought about how fortunate I was to be surrounded by so many fierce, resilient, kick-ass women.

And as I closed my eyes, I thought about how much work there was left to do, and how insurmountable it all felt. But I was comforted to think that as long as there are people willing to persevere, willing to push in pursuit of justice, there will never be a fight we cannot win.

Finally, I fell asleep.

ELEANOR CELESTE

Title: Policy Advisor for Biomedical and Forensic Sciences
Office: Office of Science and Technology Policy
Age: 27
Date: February 25, 2016

It was eleven p.m., but surprisingly, I wasn't tired. In fact, I was amped up, the kind of amped up that made me put on my headphones and walk with purpose, like I was in my own music video. To be fair, I only walked to my cab. Then from my cab up to my one-bedroom apartment in Columbia Heights, a neighborhood in Northwest Washington, DC, where my four-year-old rescue dog, Rigby, was waiting for me.

My day had started nearly eighteen hours earlier, in front of my closet, as I agonized over an outfit. I needed something that I could (1) comfortably run around in—literally, if it came to that, (2) stand in front of the President of the United States in, (3) be on camera in, and (4) not show sweat, because I inevitably sweat on big event days, even in winter.

I carefully picked a black three-quarter-sleeve knee-length dress in stretchy pique cotton with front zip pockets for my two phones—very important—and a black blazer and black tights. I looked like a well-dressed policy ninja. I finished getting ready by six-thirty a.m. By seven, I was at the office (aka the White House) to finish preparations for our largest Precision Medicine Initiative event to date.

★★★

President Obama said the words *precision medicine* for the first time in January 2015 during his State of the Union speech, when he announced the creation of the Precision Medicine Initiative (PMI). Almost overnight, the term started appearing in discussions about the future of medicine, health care, biotechnology, and pharmaceuticals. It was the cool new buzz phrase.

This is how I would explain precision medicine to a stranger in a coffee shop: Think about a disease like breast cancer. Years ago (but not that many years ago), we thought there was one type of breast cancer. Then we learned there are many types, and we can, and should, treat each case differently. Today, we can use genetic testing to find out if a patient's DNA makes them more likely to get the disease. We can also test the DNA of a tumor so doctors can determine if there is a more exact way to target it. When you have this kind of information, you can make health and lifestyle decisions based on it. That is precision medicine—using customized information, like genetics, to get the right treatment to the right person at the right time.

★★★

My journey to a career in public service started long before I ever moved to Washington and decades before POTUS launched the

Precision Medicine Initiative. The truth is I've always loved politics. I was literally born into it. In 1988, when I came into the world, my grandfather was the governor of Ohio and I was his first grandchild. As a baby and toddler, I was carried from political rallies to fund-raisers to union speeches. Then, as a middle schooler and high schooler, I stayed engaged. In my senior year of high school, I ran for class president, and I dug through my grandfather's old campaign paraphernalia to get inspiration for my posters. I ended up modeling them on a pin he had handed out on college campuses; they said *Students for Celeste, Celeste for Students.* All of this is to say that I can't remember a time when I didn't want to be involved in politics, government, or public service in some way.

I was an idealist when it came to the concept of public service. In my mind, we lived in a world where the government was an altruistic and benevolent system that was supported by people who had only the best interests of everyday citizens and our democracy at heart. Basically, I thought real life should feel like the end of an episode of *The West Wing,* or the moment in a movie where the good guys win and everyone is left with the feeling that all is right with the world. I believed, and still do, that public service is noble.

I've been fortunate to meet and work with a lot of public servants and elected officials in my life, and I have overwhelmingly found that they believe this too. Most officials take their jobs very seriously and understand the responsibility of their privileged position. They feel the weight of the letters pleading for help. They hear the voices of people who turn to them when a law or policy isn't working. They really do remember those people from the rally who couldn't work because they were struggling with cancer, or those mothers who needed access to day care so they could provide for their families. I have always found commitment to helping others through public service honorable; it's as though together we can eradicate evil by making the whole system of government better. That might sound cheesy, but it's true.

To be honest, I wasn't originally an Obama supporter. (*Gasp! I know!*) I didn't dislike him, but I was a teenage girl and there was a woman in the running for President in 2008. It was the first presidential election I got to vote in, and I loved the idea of seeing myself reflected in the highest office in our country. But when Obama won the party's nomination, I immediately threw my support behind him because I believed in both his policies and his message of hope.

I was thinking a lot about Obama's message of hope as I helped to build the Precision Medicine Initiative. But I wasn't doing it alone. I was part of a team based in the Office of Science and Technology Policy (OSTP) on the fourth floor of the Eisenhower Executive Office Building (EEOB), the big, ornate gray structure with more pillars than you can count. (It's part of the "eighteen acres," a nickname for the whole footprint of the White House complex, which literally occupies eighteen acres.)

OSTP supported the President on a number of issues, from climate change, Ebola outbreaks, and STEM education to advanced manufacturing. I focused on topics like biosecurity and science in the criminal courts—although the PMI team was definitely my favorite. It was small (six to ten people) but mighty, comprising scientists, technologists, policy wonks, and government newbies. They were my people.

In the fall of 2015, we (the PMI team) wanted to showcase our successes and bring people together to discuss solutions, so we started planning a big event at the White House, in which POTUS would participate. People don't say no to an event with President Obama.

In the year and a half since POTUS had announced PMI, a number of private-sector and nonprofit entities had committed to doing some of the hard work of moving the field of precision medicine forward, and we wanted to highlight their efforts too. For example, electronic health records were siloed within companies and even within individual doctors' offices, but the White House gathered together some of the biggest makers of electronic health records, federal government agencies, and other stakeholders, and they collectively agreed to try something new: test out sending electronic health record data directly to researchers, using computer programs. This was a big deal for those of us invested in precision medicine.

A PMI team meeting would go something like this. . . .

There would be a group of us seated around the shiny wooden table in EEOB 460. Room 460 was the conference room for OSTP; our office seal and name were mounted prominently on the wall inside the door. There was a large screen for videoconferences at the back of the room, and on the ledge by the window, there were a number of artifacts in thick plastic cases. These items were on loan to the office from other federal agencies and museums. One of them held a piece of the Allende meteorite, which contains some of the oldest matter in the known universe. It was a pretty cool and super-nerdy room—just like us.

After punching in the door code, we'd all take a seat in one of the swivel chairs at the table. Our team lead, Stephanie Devaney (Steph), probably had candy and a half-eaten scone with her, and DJ Patil, the U.S. Chief Data Scientist, would inevitably show up late, running from a meeting that required him to wear a suit and tie (a new uniform for him, coming from Silicon Valley). We'd have a short printed agenda in front of us that Steph would lead us through. Then we'd do a round-robin, which basically meant taking turns giving updates on the policies we were working on—the federal rules about how to do research with humans, the process of approving new genetic sequencing tests, the guidelines about what research information you can give back to participants, etc. Next up would be updates on activities in the private sector that were advancing precision medicine, like the formation of new companies and other large research efforts. Finally, we'd reserve the rest of the meeting to discuss the POTUS event. What should the flow of the event be? Did we think POTUS should do a speech from a podium? Or should it be a panel? Or an interview? Who should POTUS talk to? Who could interview him? Should a doctor moderate?

I would inevitably interject, "Can Mindy Kaling be included in this event somehow?" She was a TV doctor, which counts, right? We'd all end up laughing and pitching a few totally outrageous suggestions with real options mixed in. Sometimes I would feel out of place in these meetings. I wasn't a doctor or even in the medical field. I was twenty-seven years old and an attorney! Yes, I had always been interested in science. And yes, I'd studied biology at Wesleyan. And yes, I'd even studied microbiology and immunology of biohazardous threat agents and emerging infectious disease at Georgetown. But doing science policy at the White House wasn't actually part of my plan, at least not initially.

★ ★ ★

I was in the middle of law school at the Ohio State University (OSU) when my old political idealism kicked back in. I decided to accelerate my studies and finish in two and a half years instead of three so I could join a presidential campaign in 2016 (because a woman was running!). To be clear, it is not normal to finish law school early, and I needed to figure out how to get credits over the summer. OSU had a program in Washington, DC, where I could earn credit for a public service summer internship. Perfect. I had lived in DC before and still had friends there, so it would be an easy three months; then I'd go back to Ohio to finish law school and, hopefully, hop on the campaign trail with Hillary Clinton.

That summer, I applied for a bunch of positions, including an unpaid internship at OSTP in the Science Division, which I was offered and accepted. (Useful piece of advice: Do your research! Read the entire website of the place you are applying to. Let them know how interested you are. Ask real questions. Whoever is hiring likely has a thousand other responsibilities—make their job easier from the beginning and prepare.)

So how did I go from unpaid law school summer intern to full-time White House staffer? The short answer is a combination of hard work, kindness, and a touch of good luck.

Halfway through the summer, my supervisor announced she was leaving. By then, I had worked really hard to make myself a valuable part of the team, so when she suggested to both the President's Science Advisor and the Director of the Science Division that they hire me to take over parts of her job—as a White House Policy Advisor for Biomedical and Forensic Sciences— they agreed.

Holy crap!

I was still in law school, and I had a million logistics to figure out. Did I need to drop out? Take time off? Could I transfer? Could I work and simultaneously go to school? Did I have to turn down the job? How do you turn down working in the Obama White House? What about my dog? My summer sublet was ending— where would I live? Was I going to be homeless? How could I keep my work suits clean if I was homeless? These are just some of the rational and completely irrational questions and fears that raced through my mind when I was presented with the scary yet exciting choice to pivot my life and career in a way I could never have imagined just a few months earlier.

The day they officially offered me the job, I was walking home from work to my sublet in Foggy Bottom, and I called my friend who had previously worked at the White House. I told him what had happened, bursting into tears right at the corner of Twenty- Fifth and M Street NW. In that moment, I wasn't crying happy tears because working for Obama would be the coolest thing ever—I was crying because I was completely overwhelmed. (If you're so overwhelmed you could cry, I say lean into it!) Change is hard, even if it's good change, and in an instant I had to make a completely new plan for my professional future. Eventually, I pulled it together and went up to my apartment to strategize.

Step 1: Say YES to the opportunity.

Step 1.5: Fill out mountains of paperwork to get the clearances needed to work full-time in the White House.

Step 2: Figure out how to finish law school. Call OSU. *Can I finish remotely?* No. Call Washington, DC, law schools. *Do you have a nighttime program and can you take me?* (I know I missed all the deadlines, but how was I supposed to know that I would be offered a job in the frigging White House?!) Georgetown University eventually agreed to take me as a visiting student.

Step 3: Find a place to live.

Step 4: Pick up the rest of my things from Ohio. I had brought only a few suitcases' worth of summer stuff to get me through my internship, so I needed to pack up and officially move to Washington, DC.

At the end of the summer of 2015, it was official: I was the White House Policy Advisor for Biomedical and Forensic Sciences—and a full-time night student at Georgetown Law. That's when I discovered what it really meant to be busy.

★ ★ ★

At the White House, there are at least two kinds of busy: crisis busy, when you are dealing with something like the Ebola outbreak in West Africa, and event busy, when you are bringing together important, brilliant, and famous people into one of the most secure venues in the world. And when it came to events, OSTP planned some of the coolest, like the White House Science Fair, Astronomy Night, the Maker Faire, and of course, our PMI event. Planning for POTUS and two hundred guests, including members of Congress and Cabinet Secretaries, was complicated. I quickly discovered that there wasn't some well-oiled machine that does everything in the White House. Things didn't magically happen. It was just me and my team, and most of us had never planned anything more complicated than a birthday party. Luckily, there were great partners in other offices who brought expertise—like webcast, security, and sound—to certain aspects of an event. But after two-plus years at the White House, I confidently added event planning as a skill to my résumé.

Exactly one month before our big precision medicine event, on January 23, 2016, I was dealing with a very different kind of event: my mom's surgery, a double mastectomy. My mom is a breast cancer researcher, a breast cancer surgeon, the medical director of a breast program in Ohio, and now a breast cancer survivor. A disease like cancer doesn't discriminate and doesn't care if you are busy planning an event at the White House.

Sitting in the waiting room at the hospital, I kept thinking about the people who wrote letters to the President—letters about their experiences with cancer or other types of medical problems. President Obama got thousands of them every day, and an incredible team of staff and interns read, sorted, and cataloged each one. That day, I thought about those letters and about my friends and my friends' parents, who all struggled in different ways with their own cancer diagnoses. Why didn't we have better answers to why this disease strikes certain people at certain times? Why had research progressed so slowly? Would the PMI program really accelerate research and discovery the way we thought it would?

I believed in what we were building. I thought our program could create an opportunity for discovery—new science and new medicines to help people. Sometimes it felt like we were just catching up to diseases that were already winning, but at least we were trying.

That day, I also thought about how important our work was, not necessarily for my mom—who knew all the questions to ask, all the tests to order, and how to understand the results, not to mention how to navigate a broken health care system—but for each person out there who didn't know these things. We need to make the care my mom was able to advocate for herself the same care anyone would receive.

During my time on the PMI team, I talked to a lot of people who were frustrated with the health care system, and who were waiting and hoping for new and better treatments and medicines. There was one day in particular that was probably my favorite day working at the White House.

It was February 12 at ten a.m., and our event was thirteen days out. I sat down in one of the Secretary of War rooms, which are across from the Vice President's office suite in the EEOB. The

Secretary of War rooms are ornately decorated and have been well preserved since they were first occupied back in 1885—they even went through extensive restorations a few years back. The rooms are somewhat moody and dark, with elegant gold-patterned wallpaper, tufted leather couches, and heavy wooden furniture. And then there is a speakerphone with a bright green cable—the only sign of the twenty-first century.

That morning, DJ, our Chief Data Scientist, and I were stationed in the suite cold-calling people and inviting them to the White House. But not just any people . . . letter writers.

A few weeks earlier we sent an email to colleagues in the President's Correspondence Office, asking if they could search their database for letters that Americans had written to POTUS about precision medicine. We got back a PDF filled with dozens of stories, like this one, from Douglas Slemmer of Boulder, Colorado:

> I just read about the President's Precision Medicine initiative and wanted to share my thanks and our story. My wife was diagnosed 15 years ago with a rare cancer that has no proven treatment. . . . I'm in tech so for the past decade I've eagerly followed the advances in genetic profiling and targeted therapies. After pestering her doctors for years they finally informed us that there was a new genetic testing pilot program they had recommended her for. With that testing we were able to identify the two specific genetic issues driving her cancer. Knowledge in hand, we researched all available clinical trials across the nation (and world). . . . I'm thrilled to report that after 12 months of being on that trial, her tumors have been stopped,

zero growth. . . . This is the right path to finally finding effective cures.

Or this one, from Katrina Young from Carlsbad, California:

As a parent of a teenager (Sean, 17) with cystic fibrosis, I believe it is my job to ensure that all the amazing advances that we have benefited from over the past few years get into my son's hands swiftly and safely. Because of the hard work and dedication of companies like Vertex and Genetech, my son's life expectancy has increased over a decade since his diagnosis in May 2000.

Of all the health care communities, the CF Foundation best exemplifies President Obama's new precision medicine initiative. . . . [P]harmaceutical companies are hard at work figuring out the best medicinal compounds for the right person. . . . There is so much more to this disease than we currently know. And I am hopeful that programs like the precision medicine initiative will help us find those vital solutions. The important thing to keep in mind is that if we can unlock the secrets to one genetic disease, we will hold the key to curing an entire host of illnesses.

Doug and Katrina wrote to their President to share personal stories and ultimately to just say thank you. They probably never expected a response. But we were there to do more than just respond.

Our team sorted through the correspondence and identified

people who might be able to attend the event. And about two weeks before the big day, DJ and I took a seat at the wooden conference table. He had his tea; I had my coffee. Copies of the letters in hand, we dialed our first number.

The first call rang, once, twice, again, again, nothing, and then a recorded message on the other end said, "The line is full." Okay. Great start.

We tried again.

The second call started ringing, and then someone picked up. . . .

DJ: "Is this Megan?"

Voice: "Yes."

DJ: "Hi, this is DJ Patil, the President's Chief Data Scientist, and I am calling from the White House."

We could hear Megan start to giggle, not in a funny way but in a "yeah, right" way. That's often the response you get when you say you're calling from the White House. Then DJ mentioned her letter and the fact that she was a bone marrow donor. Finally, she believed him. He asked her if she would like to come to our event at the White House. "Absolutely," she replied.

We dialed a few more numbers and didn't reach anyone. Then we called Doug.

DJ: "This is DJ Patil. I am here at the White House. I am the President's Chief Data Scientist. We received your letter to the President."

Doug: [laughing] "Very good, great." (Again, I don't think he believed us.)

DJ: "How's your wife?" (Now he believed us.)

Doug: "She's doing good. . . . The trial she was on paused her cancer growth, which is phenomenal."

DJ: "That is, first and foremost, the thing I love to hear.... We want to reach out and invite you and your wife here to the White House to meet with the team and talk about your experiences and how we want to make precision medicine a reality."

When Doug told us he'd love to come, I had goose bumps all over. Doug and Katrina are like millions of other Americans who struggle when the health care system isn't giving them good answers or is leaving them feeling helpless, uncertain, or just plain confused.

We were public servants. Sure, some might say we had fancy jobs in the White House, but there was no feeling like knowing you were in the position to help someone by listening to their needs. That's when you realized that your efforts, both big and small, could change someone's life forever. Very few jobs can give you that kind of satisfaction. Public service is unique like that, and I didn't take it for granted.

That said, it is important to note that I had two super-cool job perks that my friends liked to take advantage of. First, I gave them after-hours tours of the West Wing. Second, I requested letters from the President, like the one for my friend, Haden, back home in Ohio.

Haden was fighting his own battle with the help of precision medicine. He had leukemia and was the recipient of a lifesaving transplant from an at-the-time anonymous donor from the bone marrow registry. A stranger! Haden's response to the selfless act was to set up booths at music festivals around the country to get more people signed up for the bone marrow registry. Impressed,

I wrote a note to the President's Correspondence Office and requested a letter for him.

I received Haden's note from the President a few weeks later and gave it to his mom. She framed it and presented it to him onstage at FolkFest, an event he created and curated over several years at his school in Athens, Ohio. The letter told Haden that the time he spent helping others was recognized and valued. Those simple moments, when people interacted with us, and by extension with the White House and President Obama, whether through events, letters, or phone calls, sparked something in them. Through those interactions we created ripple effects; we encouraged; we galvanized. We spread hope.

Finally, the day of our big PMI event arrived. As I woke up early to get ready, I ran through a mental checklist of all the things I had to do before it started. But I also thought about the letter writers, and the people we had called, and the visitors who would be attending that day. Would our work and our event stir something in them? Would they find it meaningful? Would we be able to inspire them?

It was only seven a.m. when I flashed my White House badge to the guard and walked through the first black iron gate that leads from Lafayette Park to West Exec Drive (the private street between the West Wing of the White House and the EEOB). I scanned my ID before passing through the metal detector and heading up West Exec toward the entrance.

I had goose bumps again, but they had nothing to do with the winter weather. Every time I approached the White House, I got that feeling. The *Is this really happening? How did I get here?* feeling. The *This is the White House and I work here!* feeling. When I started the job, someone told me that you knew it was time to leave the day that feeling wore off. That day, I wasn't at any risk of the feeling wearing off.

I went up to my office on the fourth floor. I was in before everyone else, and the only thing I needed to do was print the name tags so the interns could assemble them when they arrived. But when I sat down and put my ID card in the computer, nothing happened. *That's weird,* I thought. I tried again. Nothing. Okay, I figured IT probably sent some new software to the computers overnight. I restarted my computer and tried again. Nothing! We had a POTUS event in three hours and multiple Cabinet Secretaries were coming, and we couldn't get on our computers. Not to mention I would have to handwrite name tags for nearly two hundred people!

Crap. I started running around the halls, looking for anyone who could help. I found a coworker; her card wasn't working either. *Seriously?!* I frantically dialed the IT department, who were available around the clock for staffers having technology issues. No one was picking up. Was this a joke?

Then I started blasting text messages to friends in other White House offices, hoping someone knew a computer trick I didn't. First, I tried my friends Molly Dillon and Nita Contreras:

Me: *Our system is down!*

Me: *POTUS event at 10. Are either of you able to get on your actual computer. I know you're probably not in yet*

Me: *Yikes!!*

Me: *You're**

Me: *Of course this happens*

> **Molly Dillon:** *Ah nooo. I left my computer at wrk since I walked home in the storm. Sorry* ☹

Nita Contreras: *Also no, sorry.*

Then I tried my college friend Beck Dorey-Stein, who was a stenographer for POTUS:

Me: *You wouldn't happen to be in the office already?*

> **Beck Dorey-Stein:** *God no Im sorry! You ok?*

Me: *Our system is down. And we need to print for a 10 am POTUS event. All piv cards apparently aren't working.*

> **Beck Dorey-Stein:** *Yikes! All piv cards? Then I don't think I'd have any more luck? I'm sorry! Try staff sec? Printer shop?*

Eventually, someone from IT arrived, the system got back up and running, and at last, I clicked print on the final guest list and the formatted name tags started to roll off the printer. I carried them downstairs with a few interns to assemble at tables outside Ike's—our staff café, named for President Dwight D. Eisenhower, aka Ike—so we were closer to the room where the event would take place. I had to laugh at myself. I was a White House Policy Advisor and a lawyer assembling name tags at a café table as people like the Director of the National Institutes of Health, Cabinet Secretaries, and CEOs walked in. Welcome to the glamorous White House life! Some days I drafted policy memos for the President, and some days I tore name tags at the perforations and put them in those terrible plastic sleeves. But everyone was pitching in to make the day run smoothly, and my task was the name tags—and that was okay.

We shuttled the name tags to the sign-in table, and then I took up my position in the doorway on the right-hand side of South Court Auditorium at exactly ten a.m. Luckily, adrenaline replaced my need for more coffee.

The audience was a little antsy because they had no cell service in the room, and it was always freezing in there. I, on the other hand, was sweating, because I had been running around like a lunatic. I had my binder filled with everything I could possibly need for the event:

- The staffing plan
- Staffers' and interns' cell phone numbers
- The guest list organized by last name, by first name, and by affiliation
- The President's briefing memo
- Copies of all of our PMI policy documents

I also had the time cue cards. Yes, one of my jobs was to cue the panel. (Well, the panel moderator. Definitely not POTUS! We don't wave printed signs that say five and ten minutes remaining at POTUS. He can take as much time as he needs.) I got the text that POTUS had just walked into the clutch—what we call the time before or after an event when a select group of people gets to have a brief conversation with POTUS. Immediately, I stood up a little straighter; it was going to be only a few more minutes. Then the voice of god (VOG) came over the speakers and the audience fell silent. VOG said, "Ladies and gentlemen, the President of the United States."

Here we go, I thought.

★ ★ ★

We had decided that the format would be a panel discussion with POTUS. The moderator was a doctor and writer from the *Atlantic* named James Hamblin. The group of panelists walked onto the stage: Dr. Hamblin; POTUS; Sonia Vallabh, a lawyer turned scientist who found out she had the genetic marker for a fatal neurodegenerative disorder and gave up her law career to become a PhD student and researcher at the Broad Institute at MIT and Harvard; Howard Look, CEO of Tidepool, who built an artificial pancreas for his daughter with type 1 diabetes; and Dr. W. Marston Linehan, a researcher and physician at NIH who discovered the genetic components of kidney cancer.

My first thought was that the moderator, Dr. Hamblin, looked really young! Younger than me, for sure. Moments after the thought crossed my mind, I got a text from Beck, who was also working the event, saying, "He looks too young to get into a bar." I nearly laughed out loud and dropped my all-important time cue cards.

Dr. Hamblin was sitting to the left of POTUS, so I was definitely in both of their lines of sight, and I immediately started worrying. Would POTUS think I was trying to keep him on time? Where could I stand so it didn't look like I was waving at him? I did my best to angle myself toward the moderator and prayed I wouldn't make eye contact with POTUS while holding up a time card.

The panel started with Dr. Hamblin asking POTUS to "kick it off" by explaining why everyone was gathered that day to talk about precision medicine. The President opened his mouth and only hushed words came out. He wasn't miked! His handheld microphone was sitting on the chair behind him. It took about fifteen seconds before one of the A/V guys walked quietly onstage behind the panel and tapped POTUS on the shoulder, reaching behind his back to grab the microphone for him. The audience burst into laughter and President Obama immediately cracked a joke about the progress we had made in the "audio sciences."

The panel discussion was incredible. POTUS got an extra-big round of applause when he said that people should have control over their own health data: "I would like to think that if somebody does a test on me or my genes . . . that's mine." To have the President make a statement like that set a clear tone for where the White House stood on the issue—something my team and I would leverage as we negotiated with federal agencies and the private sector in policy discussions. (A POTUS quote is *always* helpful.)

I had successfully avoided making eye contact with President Obama while holding the time cards, but the panel had gone nearly twenty minutes over, despite my best efforts. I had gesticulated as wildly as appropriate at Dr. Hamblin, but it was a chatty panel. POTUS had staff that were responsible for getting him from scheduled meeting to scheduled meeting, and they knew he'd usually stick around when he was really invested in or moved by a meeting. Still, I hoped we hadn't derailed the President's schedule.

As soon as the audience began applauding at the end of the discussion, I crossed the room quickly to coordinate where the senior government officials were supposed to go as the event wrapped up. The panel stood up behind me on the stage and the President came off the stage to shake a few hands. I quickly stepped back against the wall, hugging my big staffing binder so he could get to the audience and his Cabinet members in the first row. He worked his way toward the exit to head back to the West Wing. As he passed by, he looked at my giant binder and shook my hand and said, "Good work." Then he disappeared through the big metal doors. That wasn't the first time I had shaken his hand, but hearing him acknowledge our efforts filled me with pride.

After POTUS exited, the audience burst into chatter. About half of the attendees stayed through the afternoon for lunch and for policy roundtable discussions led by senior Administration officials. Slowly the crowd moved from the auditorium up to the meeting rooms on the fourth floor. As the staff tried to orchestrate this migration of guests and important government officials, our PMI group message was inundated with things like "There aren't enough vegetarian lunches in EEOB 428!" and "I can't find the Cabinet Secretary, anyone have eyes on him?" and "Where can I steal more chairs for the roundtable in EEOB 442?" We had mapped out and coordinated and checked our plans for the event countless times, but we also had to be ready for the things we couldn't have predicted, like staffers grabbing the free lunches from the tables outside the rooms before our guests showed up.

That, and the fact that the President's Science Advisor, my boss, Dr. John Holdren, was pulled into an urgent meeting . . . which left me to run his policy discussion.

I found this out in approximately ten seconds before entering the room, when Dr. Holdren paused outside the door and told me that he would only be able to kick off the discussion before heading to another meeting. Honestly, there wasn't time to fully process his words.

Dr. Holdren introduced himself and had everyone around the table do the same. We had a former U.S. Chief Technology Officer in attendance, as well as presidents of nonprofits, high-ranking government officials, and patient advocates—including our letter writer Katrina and her son. They were all there to talk about privacy and security in precision medicine research. Dr. Holdren thanked the attendees for coming and then politely excused himself. When you work in the White House, there is always a more important meeting going on somewhere, so you could never fault someone for making an early exit. He could have been going to meet with POTUS, for all we knew.

I stood at the front of the room and began the discussion.

Over the previous year, I had led a team in drafting and finalizing two cornerstone policy documents: the Privacy and Trust Principles and the Data Security Policy Principles and Framework, both related to precision medicine. Prior to the event, we had released, for the first time, the draft of the data security document. This discussion was a chance for me to collect initial feedback from some of the smart and important people who had traveled to DC for our event. I was excited to hear people's reactions to something I had worked so hard on, but I was also a little nervous—not for the feedback but that the discussion wouldn't flow and that people would find it boring. For me, there is nothing worse than a totally vanilla meeting that feels like a waste of everyone's time.

Luckily, it wasn't boring, vanilla, or anywhere close to it. People were animated and impressed that the first policies the team tackled were privacy and data security. It was valuable to have Katrina and her son there; they provided perspective on what it was like to have to advocate for lifesaving care day to day. I left the discussion proud of the work my team and I had done. We were making progress—I wasn't sure where it was going to lead at that moment, but it felt like we were moving forward.

Planning and executing an event with the President moved our policy agenda forward, but it also brought attention to the topic of precision medicine. The *New York Times* headline read "President Weighs in on Data from Genes," while the *Wall Street Journal* said "U.S. 'Precision Medicine' Study Seeks Genetic Patterns of Disease." After a busy and emotional day, it was gratifying to see positive press coverage.

Our team was scrolling through the headlines that were already online as we walked to a bar near the White House to celebrate and unwind. We had anticipated the need for a post-work gathering and planned for everyone to meet upstairs at the Hamilton, just a few blocks away.

I texted Haden's mom to tell her about the event; I also told her I was thinking about her son. (Haden passed away in December 2016. His efforts to get more people onto the bone marrow registry continue at music festivals around the country in his honor, his letter from President Obama sat on the entry table at his end-of-life celebration as one of his favorite things.)

And then I called my mom. I know, very uncool. But I wasn't calling because I was feeling emotional or proud or because in that moment I was thinking about how she was doing (which I was—all three!). I called my mom to tell her that the Director of the National Institutes of Health, one of the top geneticists in the *whole world,* was sitting against the back wall of the upstairs bar at the Hamilton, singing an original song he wrote about precision medicine. Yes, Dr. Francis Collins graced the staff and guests with not one but *two* original songs. I wanted desperately to Facetime with her so she could experience it, but that might have been too much. Instead, I called her from the corner so she could hear a bit of the song while I looked like I was doing something important.

While I was talking to her, I got that feeling again. The same feeling I got every morning when I walked through those heavy metal gates into the White House complex. *Is this real life? How did I get so lucky to be in this room, with such accomplished, smart people, just letting loose? Why me?*

It was one of those days when everything collides—months of work, incredible people, personal stuff, and my idealism about government.

Standing in the corner of the bar, calling my mom back in Ohio, I thought, *This is why I love public service.* It was hard and sweaty and I totally kicked ass.

Then I thought, *I can't wait to do it again tomorrow.*

Backstage with some of the *Annie* crew. Left to right: Director Will Gluck, Molly Dillon, Quvenzhané Wallis, Rose Byrne (front), Cameron Diaz, Daniel Dominguez (Bobby Cannavale's cousin), Bobby Cannavale, and Jamie Foxx.

A screenshot of the foster care event's live stream, broadcast to the world on WhiteHouse.gov. Molly Dillon welcomes Vice President Biden and his daughter Ashley to the stage.

Molly Dillon volunteering at Halloween on the South Lawn, a few weeks before the *Annie* event.

In celebration of her twenty-fifth birthday and the passage of Senate bill S.744, Andrea R. Flores blows out candles.

Andrea R. Flores at her desk in the immigration office.

Andrea R. Flores standing outside 708 Jackson Place, the home of the White House immigration team.

First Lady Michelle Obama and the Mathtastic 4 (in purple tutus!) at the United State of Women Summit.

Amanda Lucidon

Mikaila Ulmer and President Barack Obama backstage at the United State of Women Summit.

Kalisha Dessources
Figures (right) and
her partner in crime,
Jordan Brooks.

Kelly Jo Smart

Kalisha Dessources Figures (third from left) takes her mom, dad, and three
sisters to the Oval Office for her departure photo, a few months before the
end of the Administration.

Chuck Kennedy

After Easter church service in 2014. Taylor Lustig mainly had this photo taken to show her family what she wore to church with POTUS and family.

This pope survival pack, including a pope on a Popsicle stick, appeared on Taylor Lustig's desk the day before the papal visit, courtesy of her friend Molly Dillon.

Taylor Lustig, packed up and ready to head out the door on her last night on the job. The "jumbos" decorating her office included one of the pope petting Bo (behind Taylor) and one of President Obama wearing a yarmulke (left against the wall). It was the faith office, after all.

Dr. Raúl Plascencia, then President of Mexico's National Commission on Human Rights, addresses the audience while Vivian P. Graubard waits to give her speech.

U.S. State Department

The talavera cross given to Vivian P. Graubard at TechCamp in Tlaxcala, Mexico.

Vivian P. Graubard and her two younger brothers, Christian (left) and Hans (right), stand in front of the West Wing.

Yara Shahidi watches President Obama deliver remarks at the White House Science Fair in the East Room of the White House.

The panel discussion on precision medicine in the auditorium of the Eisenhower Executive Office Building. Eleanor Celeste took this photo from the corner where she was cuing the moderator with time cards. Moderator: Dr. James Hamblin. Panelists from left to right: President Barack Obama, Sonia Vallabh, Howard Look, and Dr. W. Marston Linehan.

President Barack Obama and First Lady Michelle Obama greet people arriving on Martha's Vineyard, including Eleanor Celeste's sisters, Julia Celeste and Anna Viragh (in foreground).

White House Photo Office

Eleanor Celeste outside her office in the Eisenhower Executive Office Building.

Melanie Lynch

Nita Contreras prepares to board Air Force One on her first presidential trip, to New Orleans.

Nita Contreras in front of "the Beast" (President Obama's limo) in the Treme neighborhood of New Orleans.

A typical in-flight work setup for Nita Contreras. Nita took this photo en route from Joint Base Andrews to Springfield, Illinois.

White House film festival invitations laid out the night before the event.

The White House film festival stage in the East Room, with emcees Terrence J and Kal Penn.

Jenna Brayton (right) and Hilary Swank (left) in the White House Press Briefing Room at the end of the West Wing tour.

Jaimie Woo outside Air Force Two, right before takeoff at
Joint Base Andrews.

Jaimie Woo's parents
meeting Vice President
Joe Biden. Her mom
had that expression the
entire time.

David Lienemann

A cancer policy briefing with the Vice President in his West Wing office. Pictured are Doug Lowy, Acting Director of the National Cancer Institute (on couch by Jaimie Woo), Thomas Kalil, Deputy Director for Policy of the White House Office of Science and Technology Policy (left), and Don Graves (right). Notice the binders on Jaimie's lap and on the couch. Not pictured: two more binders on the floor by her feet.

David Lienemann

The Domestic Policy Council Policy Assistants in October 2014, right before Noemie C. Levy left the department and changed roles in the White House. Noemie is in front, and her friends and coworkers Molly Dillon (far left) and Taylor Lustig (far right) are in the second row.

The White House Office of Social Innovation and Civic Participation team photo, with Noemie C. Levy, at Camp David.

Noemie C. Levy and her family share their immigration story with President Obama in the Oval Office on March 6, 2016, three months before she left the White House.

Pete Souza

My job at the White House, at least on the surface, seemed simple: I was charged with putting together the President's Daily Briefing Book. And by briefing book, I mean a very organized, fancy leather binder with color-coded folders containing the presidential papers: a memorandum for each of the next day's events, trip itineraries, ten LADs (Letters a Day, written to the President by ordinary citizens), speeches, and priority decision and briefing memos from senior White House staff. Each type of document had its place, with a specific format and corresponding-color folder. Part of the job for my six-person office was to make sure the staff who wrote these papers were consistent and clear. The other big responsibility was reading everything carefully in order to edit and finalize the multitude of pages that went to the President's desk every night in preparation for the following day. It could be exhausting at times—scanning page after page of similar drafts of the same thing. *The President stands here; at this time he says x; then he leaves by exiting stage y.* But that was my job—to ensure the content was accurate and the formatting and punctuation were uniform on every page. While this might sound boring, it was critical that his book—and the information it contained—be flawlessly accurate. As a bonus, the content was consistently interesting and at times even thrilling. For instance, I got to read drafts of the White House Correspondents' Dinner speech before anyone else, and I knew ahead of time whether the monthly jobs report was promising or concerning. I saw firsthand the enormous amount of work that goes into every presidential trip—foreign or domestic—to advance the Administration's policies.

This was not an easy job, even for someone like me, a perfectionist by nature. I wanted to be perfect so that I could make the

NITA CONTRERAS

Title: Assistant Staff Secretary
Office: Office of the Staff Secretary
Ages: 25–27
Dates: August 27, 2015
February 12, 2016
April 25, 2016
November 2, 2016

Working at the White House may be a dream for many, but it wasn't my dream, at least not initially. I didn't grow up in a political household, I didn't study politics, and until Barack Obama ran for President, I didn't have any interest in politics. But as an eighteen-year-old Latina and a first-time voter, I could not wait to cast my ballot for our first African American president. I was unbelievably excited to celebrate with droves of my fellow college students the night he was elected—his victory made me feel like anything was possible, especially for a young woman of color like me.

Little did I know, the real excitement was still to come. After a call for résumés at my college, I was invited to interview in Washington, DC, upon my graduation. More exciting still was being hired as a political appointee in Obama's Administration at the U.S. Department of Agriculture (USDA). But the pinnacle of my young career came after three and a half years, when I was offered a job in the West Wing of the White House. *Me?*

President's job just a tiny bit easier. That doesn't mean I didn't make my fair share of mistakes; however, I was fortunate enough to work in an office with a supportive boss and team, and for a president who provided a safe space not only to fail but to own up to—and grow from—my mistakes. I learned humility in the face of power and gratitude for being trusted with such an enormous responsibility while never having to compromise myself, my beliefs, or my feeling of self-worth.

That doesn't mean I didn't get caught up sometimes in the craziness of the West Wing. I made mistakes, but those experiences taught me the biggest lessons—ones that are worth sharing.

August 27, 2015
Five months into my job, I got to take my first trip with the President—to New Orleans, a place I'd never been before. The trip marked the ten-year anniversary of Hurricane Katrina, and we were going to check on recovery efforts and rebuilt neighborhoods. After months of sightings and near run-ins around the West Wing, I finally got to travel with POTUS.

I planned for this day for weeks: what I was going to wear, what I would say, how I would remain calm, cool, and collected. I didn't sleep much the night before—all I could think about was how to prepare, how not to make a mistake. Everything needed to be absolutely *perfect.*

I got to work early the morning of our departure. I grabbed the biggest coffee the Navy Mess carried (gotta be alert!), double-checked that I had everything packed, and printed as much book material in advance as I could. Planning ahead comes in handy when you're on the road, because there are plenty of opportunities for missteps. Between stops, I was trying to edit, hole-punch, organize, and not spill, rip, or otherwise damage the more than sixty pages the President would personally read and mark up each night. There wasn't much to print yet (not many event memos are submitted before the deadline), so I ticked through my packing list again to make sure I had a binder, an ethernet cord, a hole punch, label sheets, paper clips, pens of every color, and, well, you get the picture. . . .

While this may seem like unnecessary overpreparation (and, let's face it, overpacking), it's important to understand that most trips were spent on the go. We were carted around in large vans, and I often stood and waited in tiny spaces, trying to stay out of the way. More often than not, I scrambled around makeshift offices, racing against time (and sometimes printers) to get every-thing ready before boarding the plane again. We even carried a portable printer, aka "Printy," with us at all times. Literally every. Single. Trip. Printy may have been the most valuable member of the team.

By the time I walked out of the office, I looked like a bag lady. Printy, portable office, and purse in one hand and an extra-large coffee in the other, I rolled out with my boss, Joani Walsh, to West Exec, a street that isn't really a street, which separates the West Wing from the Eisenhower Executive Office Building (EEOB) and is where senior staff park. I felt pretty good, like I'd already nailed the trip, when all I'd accomplished was getting myself out the door on time. But the excitement of so many firsts triggered my adrenaline, as did the nerves about getting everything right.

We loaded into one of the unmarked black vans idling out front, just past where the Vice President's limo parked every morning. After a quick head count, the vans departed. As we passed through gate after gate of security and exited the complex,

I thought, *I can't believe I work at the White House. I can't believe I work for the President of the United States.* It was a complete shock not only to me but to those closest to me. My ambition never came as a surprise to my parents, one an immigrant and both public school teachers, but I don't think anything could have prepared them for where my path would lead. I was in awe of my job, of my role in the first black president's administration. Thanks to them, thanks to a family that has always put me first, endlessly supported me, and pushed me to succeed, I arrived at the White House. It's hard to describe; the sensation hit me in unexpected waves. It was a feeling that made me stand up a little straighter and recognize the weight of my privilege and responsibility and feel . . . *all* the feels.

After an uneventful thirty-minute drive, we arrived at Joint Base Andrews. We passed through more layers of security. I had never been on a military base, and suddenly realized the distinct similarities to where I worked—armed guards waved us through as we drove into a much larger version of the secure complex I was still getting used to.

Before I knew it, we'd reached the final security gate leading out to the airfield, and then we were on the tarmac. We passed some small military planes; a few had "United States of America" painted on them in capital navy blue letters, which popped against the baby blue, royal blue, and white background. We stopped in front of a large 747, and it felt like we were on a movie set—but it was real. *It's actually happening,* I thought. It was barely ten in the morning, and I couldn't imagine my life getting any better than this moment. Maybe I didn't need so much coffee after all!

Stepping out of the van, I collected my things, and my composure, while momentarily staring at the stunning and awe-inspiring plane: Air Force One. Nothing can prepare you for this moment. Standing in front of the most famous airplane in the world, knowing you're about to board. We unloaded on the tarmac in front of a large, red velvet–covered staircase. Literally a red carpet! Uniformed marines waited at the bottom to inspect the pin I wore proudly and prominently, a blue hexagon that marked me as a staff member and allowed me past rope lines and into the President's space, and to make sure I was manifested (aka on the list). Fun fact: It's not technically AF1 until the President boards.

Joani, who noticed my unusual silence and unwavering grin, asked, "Want a picture?"

"No, I'm good. Taking plenty of mental pictures," I said stupidly. I was trying to seem professional and not let on to the fact that I was totally fangirling out.

"No, really, go take a picture."

"It's your first trip?" Sarada Peri, a presidential speechwriter, asked, walking up, but she could already tell. "Take some pictures." Here I was trying to play it cool, but these women knew better: no one is too cool for Air Force One.

Twenty-five pictures of me at various stages of my ascent up the staircase later, I took my first peek inside. To say it's breathtaking is an understatement—and that's not because it's flashy or over-the-top. It's really not. It's beautiful because it's like no other plane you'll ever be on. I wandered past the President's conference room and a constantly restocked bowl of fresh fruit to find my seat (which was assigned, by the way, with a quarter sheet of paper bearing my name, the Presidential Seal, and a nice little printed message that said "Welcome Aboard Air Force One" propped up on the wood-paneled armrest).

An announcement let us know that the President was en route. He, unlike us, does not arrive by car (unless the weather is bad). Instead, he touched down at Andrews after a ten-minute flight from the White House South Lawn aboard the presidential helicopter, Marine One (also named Marine One only once the President boards).

I jumped up out of my seat to huddle at the windows on the left side—along with the videographer and a few other staff—to catch a glimpse of these incredible helicopters landing (Marine One and its escorts) and to watch the President disembark, wave at the press gathered outside, and board AF1.

Soon after, we were off, and it was back to business. My boss explained our strategy as we pored over the mini schedules we'd been handed. We talked through how to make a game plan, identifying where to print the briefing book pages and when. I was only slightly distracted by spotting my name on the manifest for AF1, and in the official schedule, for everyone to see. *I'm keeping this forever,* I thought as I heard Joani say, ". . . and don't forget to board the motorcade *before* the President. Know which van you're going to and get in quickly or you *will* be left behind. . . ."

It's happened to others, even the most senior staff. We've all heard the stories. The motorcade waits for only one person.

Three things stood out to me from that first flight.

1. There's no safety demonstration—it's assumed you know what to do, but also, the plane is incredibly safe. I don't know all the numerous ways it's protected, but it is. I have no idea if there are even life vests or oxygen bags on board. And no one tells you to turn off your cell phone.

2. There's no real warning for takeoff. Three bells ring, and then—rapid acceleration. Some seasoned travelers even "surf" (stay standing) on the takeoff (for fun).

3. If you are ever on AF1, CALL EVERYONE YOU KNOW. (Well, maybe not everyone, because it costs money, but you get the idea.) When you get a phone call from the plane, an actual operator tells you that you have an incoming call from Air Force One before they connect you. And it never stops being cool to be able to make those calls. I used the unclassified phone at my seat to call my parents. And my best friend, Caitlin. (But I'll never reveal in which order.)

I wanted to savor every moment. To bottle up the whole day and keep it with me. But there were four moments I knew I would never forget.

1. A POTUS Motorcade

The motorcade ride was my favorite part of the trip. I didn't often get to ride in fancy cars at the U.S. Department of Agriculture (USDA), but on one particular trip in an official vehicle, my boss's driver used his police light to clear traffic. It was exhilarating, since I'd never experienced anything like it, and it made me feel important. That, however, paled in comparison to being in a presidential motorcade. In New Orleans, so many people gathered to wave at President Obama. People even jumped out of their stopped cars to take photos and videos as we passed. And it was clear that all this commotion was not just about a presidential motorcade, but about *this* particular president. The mere hope of catching a glimpse of the car (aka "The Beast") transporting Barack Obama (the bulletproof-glass windows are tinted, so you can't really see his face) was enough to make people wait for hours. You could sense the energy as we passed miles of people—some stretches populated two to three rows deep—and it almost brought tears to my eyes. I felt their excitement, remembering when I first moved to DC and worked at the USDA and my mom came to visit. We were leaving USDA's headquarters on the National Mall when the presidential motorcade drove by; my mom waved and to this day swears that the President waved back at her. For so many of the people we were passing, this was the closest they would ever get to him. Many of us waved back (even though they were obviously looking for a wave from POTUS, not us) and watched people's reactions. Their joy was infectious.

2. A Neighborhood Stroll

Our first stop was in a neighborhood called Treme. We were visiting housing that had been rebuilt after Hurricane Katrina. When the motorcade stopped, the President got out of his car and began to walk house to house, knocking on doors and asking people about their new homes and lives. (If the walk hadn't been planned in advance, this would have freaked out the Secret Service.) Staff were given the option to follow at a distance. I leapt from the van and kept a close tail. More than a few residents were shocked to see POTUS on their front steps, just there to have a conversation. He shook hands with many and embraced others, but my favorite part was when he squatted down to say hello to a little boy wearing Dalmatian-spotted pajamas and Spider-Man Crocs, coaxing him out from behind his mother's legs by offering him a box of presidential M&M's. The boy couldn't have been more than three, but POTUS was just as engaged with that tiny boy, who may or may not have known that he was talking to the leader of the free world, as he was with a grandmother who had lived through Katrina.

3. The President's Words

I loved watching the President deliver his speech at the Andrew P. Sanchez Community Center. We got to hide backstage and peek through the curtains, listening and feeling the crowd's energy from behind the scenes. Obama speaks with such emotion, it's almost preacherlike. The New Orleans crowd rose and fell with his words. I could see people smile and tear up from my secret vantage point. And my favorite line of that speech, about New Orleans and its place as the "gateway to America's soul," is a line I'll never forget: "The jazz makes you cry, the funerals make you dance, and the bayou makes you believe all kinds of things." I felt the spirit of the city and the mission of the President aligning in that moment.

4. The Mistake with a Capital M

Besides getting to enjoy the President's presence and energy, my reason for being on any trip is to put together his book. After printing as much of the proofread and edited material as we could, my boss and I loaded the motorcade. We were in pretty good shape, we decided, and laid out a plan to finish the book on the plane. Since this was my first book on the road, Joani reminded me that it was more important to make sure the final product was right than to rush to get it to POTUS as soon as possible. (The goal was usually to hand over the book before, or as soon as, we board.)

So when we arrived at the plane, we unpacked all the book's components and started assembling it as we waited for the schedule to go final (meaning pencils down, no more changes to be made). The "book" was usually a nice thick leather binder with the Presidential Seal on the front, framed with gold metal corners. It was probably about an inch thick most days. Some days, there was more going on in the world, which meant more papers for the President to read and a bigger binder to hold them all. I made sure that there were labels on each event tab, that the memos were in the correct colored folders, and that bios, speeches, and decision tabs were where they all belonged. We paged through the book one final time.

"Ready?" Joani asked.

"I think so," I said as my heart started to beat faster. I realized that this was the moment I was about to walk into the President's conference room and be formally introduced.

I was escorted to the room, where the President was already seated. A game of spades was about to begin.

The President's trip director introduced me: "This is Nita. She works in Staff Sec. She came to us from the USDA."

"Hi, Nita, it's nice to meet you. Thanks for coming to work for us," President Obama said. (At least, I think he said something like that; I can't remember because I was too excited.) He was looking right at me in an intense but kind way. Meanwhile, I was thinking, *Shit shit shit, I'm literally talking to the leader of the free world. And now he knows my name.*

"Here's your book for tomorrow, sir," I said, and without

actually breaking into a run, I bolted for the door as quickly as I could. I got back to the staff area and sat down next to Joani.

"How'd it go?" she asked.

"He knows my name," I said breathlessly.

At that moment, dinner was delivered. It was lovely; the military chefs plan a themed meal to correspond with each trip. That day we had jambalaya with jalapeño corn bread, a wedge salad with bacon, and lemon bars—all this on top of the fried chicken I'd wolfed down like it was my job during our lunch stop at Willie Mae's. I wasn't hungry, but at the same time, I was—all the nervous energy and adrenaline had left me with a healthy appetite. We were also served a beverage of our choice. I chose white wine, because it was after seven p.m. and I needed something to calm me down after that wave of emotion and anxiousness. Plus, I got to drink wine from an AF1-etched glass on AF1. Enough said.

As I took a sip, I saw the President's aide walk into my seating area. He headed over to my boss and whispered something in her ear. Immediately, all my calm was gone. When he walked away, I asked Joani, "What's wrong?"

"Nothing."

"No, something's wrong. What did I do?"

"It's fine, I'll fix it."

"No," I said, pushing past the nerves. I needed to fix whatever mistake I'd made. "I gave him the book. If you go in and fix it, he'll think I'm too scared to own up to my mistakes. Let me do it, please."

Turns out it wasn't the biggest mistake I'd ever made; it just happened to be in very plain view of the Boss. I had delivered the wrong schedule. It's confusing to constantly work on the day ahead. Everything around us, including the schedule I'd stared at all day to make sure it didn't get lost or left behind, said it was August 27, 2015, while the product I put together should have said August 28, 2015. It was a rookie mistake but an easy one to make. I printed the correct schedule and put it into a folder.

"Just walk it in and leave it on the corner of the table."

"Okay," I said, embarrassed and slightly terrified.

I wasn't *so* concerned about the mistake itself—it was small and they happen. It was an unfortunate but good reminder to take my time. I was more worried about the disappointment. I'd been hired to take on this incredible responsibility, and I hadn't quite met the mark.

I walked in and made a beeline for the end of the table farthest from the President, where his aide was sitting. As I stooped over to explain that *this* was the correct schedule, the President looked up, and our eyes met. To my surprise, he broke into a big smile. It said *I know you gave me today's schedule instead of tomorrow's,* and I chose to think he was smiling because he was happy that I'd come back in to fix the error. I couldn't help but smile too.

"Here's your *actual* schedule for tomorrow, sir," I said, know- ing I'd been caught trying to drop off the corrected version before he saw me. I kept direct eye contact as I walked over and handed him the folder. I tried to act like I wasn't ashamed, even though I was.

He started to laugh, and I smiled bigger. For a moment, we shared this incredible bond of understanding. He wasn't perfect; he had made mistakes before. And while being handed today's schedule instead of tomorrow's might throw some bosses into a rage, that wasn't something he was going to get worked up over.

I walked back out of the conference room and felt a real victory. Not the "I've won the day and it's only nine a.m." victory I'd felt that morning, but one I knew my parents would be proud of.

If I had any worry that the President would soon forget who I was, I was certain that goofing up on my first trip would make me memorable. I was able to enjoy the rest of the flight home. A few sent emails later, my work was done.

After we landed, I collected my First Flight certificate (yes, they make those for AF1, like commercial airlines do when children fly for the first time) and other mementos from the trip. I watched the President take off in Marine One and then vanned it back to the White House. I dropped and unpacked my bags in the office and said hello to the coworker who had been my teammate back at the office on this adventure. I gave a few brief highlights of the day, including the motorcade and meeting the President, with the promise of more to come in the morning—including the story of fixing my mistake.

All in all, getting home before midnight wasn't even a long day. But I was exhausted. I'd been exhausted for months. Still, on days like that, days when I remembered my imperfections and realized that I could do something dumb without it meaning *I* was dumb, when I could pick myself up after an embarrassing mistake and still feel like I belonged on the team . . . well, days like that made the exhaustion, the missed phone calls, the forgotten birthdays, and everything else feel worth it.

I was living the dream.

February 12, 2016
On my first "long" trip (more than one night), I had another really big first. Not only did I get to fly out of my hometown airport

and over my childhood home in a super-cool military helicopter on a beautiful California day, but after nearly a year at the White House, working a job that used all my time and energy and often made it hard for me to see my family, my parents got to meet the President.

I'd been looking forward to this trip, knowing that there would be a small chance I could get my parents into a photo line. At most events, the President makes time to take photos with people, but the list is usually pretty short. I'd waited patiently, knowing that you only get one big ask. I was going to save mine for something really, really good. When scheduling told us about this stop, I knew my moment had come—I excitedly called my parents to invite them to Westwood, California. My dad grumbled slightly about having to miss work.

"But, Dad, it's to meet the President of the United States. Barack Obama?"

"And?" said Dad.

Did I make clear that I was bursting at the seams that I'd made this moment possible, and my dad's mild disinterest totally deflated my happy balloon?

"It would mean a lot to me," I said, "but it's your choice."

My mom, on the other hand, needed no convincing. She would have traveled to any city to make this happen. But the real miracle is that she managed to drag my dad along. My parents are both teachers, so they called in subs, went through the effort of crafting lesson plans, found parking (which can feel pretty near impossible on a busy day in Westwood), and showed up at the hotel in coordinating outfits. (Thanks, Mom!)

After getting myself packed, dressed, and ready for my last "work" day of the trip, I met my parents and brought them upstairs to line up for their picture with POTUS. We got checked in, meaning I said hi to my coworkers Emily Boyle and Bobby Schmuck, who had organized the event, and introduced them to my parents. This was basically my version of "bring your child to work day," but in reverse. As the line began to move, I left my parents, who at this point had a clear understanding of their instructions (stay in line, don't embarrass me), to head to the motorcade.

I was adding on a short visit home after our last stop, so I told them, "I'll see you tomorrow," before gathering my carry-on, purse, and classified bag (where the mobile office lives) and hobbling off under the weight of all three. My parents were driving out to Palm Springs to pick me up after I ended my on-duty part of the trip— a three-hour drive each way, so no small journey for them. Turns out you're never too old to be picked up by Mom and Dad.

I loaded up the van and chatted with some folks as we waited for the go-ahead.

My work phone rang. It was Bobby.

"Where are you?" he asked.

"At the motorcade."

"But your parents are up here."

"Yeah, are they doing okay?"

"Of course. But you should be here, in the photo with them."

"Oh." That hadn't occurred to me. "Are you sure?" As presidential staffers, we were pretty much trained to think that it was never about us. It was about the mission and the office and the President. We were the behind-the-scenes crew. We were public servants.

"It's a chance for POTUS to meet *your* family. You have to come up!"

There was no time to argue. I asked one of the military aides to watch my bags for the next five minutes and ran back inside—just in time.

Bobby introduced my parents to POTUS. My parents stepped up to shake his hand.

"We're very lucky to have Nita. She's doing a great job," POTUS told them.

They beamed, said something that I'm sure was polite, admiring but still appropriate (their exact words escape me, I was so caught up in the moment), while Pete Souza, the President's photographer, motioned us into a pose, arranging my dad at my side and putting my mom on the other side of POTUS. I could tell she was trying to hold back tears at this point. It was a dream come true—for all of us.

Before we knew it, the photo op was over and we walked outside.

Unable to fully process that we'd just taken a family photo (except for my brother, who was at school in Boston) with the President, I turned to my parents and told them, "Okay, gotta run! They only hold the motorcade for one person—and that person is not me."

My mom started to tear up. "He's proud of you! So are we," she said, hugging me.

Seeing my mom cry, even out of happiness, shook me. But there was no time for tears. I kissed them both and ran away before I started to cry too. I was still on duty, after all, and I felt like I probably should not cry at work. Even if my mom was there crying.

We loaded the motorcade, and I waved goodbye to my parents and other onlookers; then we were off.

As we approached my hometown airport—tiny and about a mile from the Pacific Ocean—I was soaring. And I still sort of felt like crying. Pulling myself together, I joined my coworkers as we transferred to helicopters, which is truly the fastest way to travel around LA. The crew even left the backs of the helicopters open, and I got a beautiful photo of my hometown as we flew toward LAX. Growing up in Santa Monica, I never imagined getting to fly over my city in a military helicopter after introducing my parents to the President. I couldn't have dreamed it if I'd tried.

We landed at LAX and boarded AF1, and at that point, I was focused solely on putting together the book, albeit a short one, for a low-key weekend. (Or so I thought—Supreme Court Justice Antonin Scalia passed away that weekend, and we scrambled to do a last-minute press conference minutes before my on-duty portion of the trip ended.) Instead of heading for my seat, I ran around printing and hole-punching things as we waited for POTUS to wave to the press and board. While I was doing my double check, I looked up to see POTUS walking by. He was heading back to the guest cabin, where some friends were waiting—they were joining him for a weekend of golf before the Association of Southeast Asian Nations (ASEAN) Summit began on Monday. I looked back down.

"It was really nice to meet your folks," he said, catching me off guard.

"Thank you, sir," I replied, pausing from my task and looking up again to catch his eye. And then he kept moving, and so did I. After all, I had a briefing book to finish.

April 25, 2016
An OCONUS (Outside the Contiguous U.S., or overseas) trip is something every staffer looks forward to. I'd been waiting for my chance since the day I started. It's a whirlwind of countries,

speeches, and important meetings, and the chance to explore somewhere new on a much greater scale than on a domestic trip. The tiredness I saw on the face of coworkers returning from an OCUNUS didn't deter me. I love travel—even the stressful kind—and I'd been presented with a once-in-a-lifetime opportunity.

Since my boss and I were both going and there was limited seating, given the approximately eighty staff traveling with us, I would fly not on AF1 but on a separate staff plane. I was hoping for a quiet, uneventful, and relaxing ride, because I knew that whatever followed the flight would be anything but calm.

We would be visiting three countries in six days: twenty-four hours in Saudi Arabia, the weekend in the UK, and thirty-six hours in Germany. Preparation for this trip had pushed my type-A personality to another level. I had a carry-on bag with an eye mask and a neck pillow, comfortable but coworker-appropriate pajamas, melatonin, chamomile tea—everything I could think of to help an insomnia-prone twenty-six-year-old get some much-needed rest on the thirteen-hour flight. I was even short and small enough to fit on the bench in the small plane's conference room, so I had the luxury of lying down on a nonfloor surface. Score!

Despite all my preparations, however, sleep never really came. This trip was going to be unforgettable, and the excitement made me restless. Traveling with the President meant access to amazing sites and experiences I'd never get to have again. At noon AST/5:00 a.m. EST, about an hour and a half before landing, I begrudgingly gave up on sleep and waited in line for the bathroom to put on my "loose-fitting but head-to-toe covering" attire for the ninety-degree heat of Riyadh. I had literally one outfit in my closet that covered my wrists, neck, and ankles without being too formfitting. It's all about the small victories.

However, the day in Saudi Arabia didn't go according to plan. I was surprised to see tanks outside the hotel upon our arrival—definitely not something you usually see in the United States. And while the hotel staff were incredibly friendly, some of the guests were less than pleased to witness two unaccompanied women (my boss and me) grabbing coffee (just coffee!) in the hotel lobby while we waited for final book materials that evening.

And then there was dinner. While Joani and I had heard about a phenomenal place just a few miles from the hotel, by the time we'd put together the book and delivered it, most of the other staff had already left for their dinner plans. That left two women who would need to be escorted to dinner (us), and by the time we contemplated the abayas (traditional loose-fitting garments for women, covering them from neck to toe) that advance had on-site for us, plus how to arrange a driver, it felt like more effort and stress than it was worth for a meal when we would be getting up early anyway. Resigned, we went to the hotel restaurant, where the lack of women continued to be apparent. Our server, a friendly man from Indonesia, explained to us that Saudi Arabia had to bring in men from other countries to do jobs you might see women doing in the States—waiting tables, cleaning, etc. Again, we stuck out like sore thumbs.

The next morning, still confused by our experiences the night before, I was extremely cautious about covering myself up for a trip to the women's hotel gym. Since my boss would be accompanying POTUS on the day's stops, I was able to have a slower morning—breakfast with some coworkers, followed by a quick workout—before paper started flowing again. After finding the gym and stripping off my sweatshirt and sweatpants to the workout clothes I'd worn underneath—items appropriate for a workout in the desert heat—I went for a short run on the treadmill and then back to my room. As I was stepping out of the shower, I got a call from my boss, who had loaded up the motorcade—but Printy was still in the SCIF (Sensitive Compartmented Information Facility)! On a foreign trip, essentially all of our work, classified or not, is done in a SCIF, built by White House staff in hotel rooms wherever we're staying, to ensure privacy.

POTUS was on his way down to the motorcade, and since we know the motorcade waits for only one person, it was up to me to bring Printy down. Only problem was, I was still in a towel.

Heart thumping, I dressed quickly. The on-site printers had been less than reliable the day before, so without Printy, there was no backup printer. I zipped up my heeled boots (did I mention that the only pants I have that fit the Saudi requirement were hemmed for heels, and that without heels, I would surely trip over the bottoms while running?) and ran full speed down the length of the hallway, pausing to show Secret Service my pin as I entered the restricted wing. I ran down some more hallway and into the SCIF, grabbed Printy, and rushed back out toward the elevators. I momentarily contemplated whether I could run down eight flights of stairs faster than waiting for the elevator.

Shit, I thought, *where is the motorcade?*

I hadn't grabbed the mini schedule in my haste, and remembered vaguely that the motorcade was not outside the main hotel entrance. I stopped in the lobby and caught someone on the advance team. She told me to take the stairs down to the basement, and it would be at the end of the long hall. I breathlessly thanked her and continued on my sprint—wet hair, pre-makeup, post-run, panting. If they were surprised to see women ordering coffee, I can only imagine what people thought about me now.

Miraculously, I made it to the motorcade before POTUS. My boss thanked me, and I began my walk back up, finally catching my breath . . . only to realize that the hall I had come through was exactly the one (because it was the only one) POTUS would be using to head toward the motorcade. And it was just my luck that he happened to be walking toward me at that exact moment. I stopped walking, hoping I might blend into the wall instead of being spotted by the leader of the free world looking my *most* disheveled. I combed my wet hair with my fingers and straightened my blouse, while at the same time trying to take up as little space as possible and avoid eye contact, which proved difficult because it wasn't just the President but his aides and senior staff walking the width of the hallway. I had nowhere to escape to, and of course the President misses nothing. He looked at me slightly puzzled, said good morning, and continued walking. Mission accomplished.

The London portion of this trip wasn't without its ups and downs either. The support plane staff were stranded at Stansted Airport due to a miscommunication, so the vans left without us. Plus, we landed to the news that Prince had died, so the mood was somber.

But the next day was looking up. With the trip to Windsor Castle extremely limited, staffwise, my boss and I got to spend the day exploring London together. After a few goofy photos around touristy sites and even more touristy stops for tea and presents for our office mates (a requirement enforced by all Staff Sec not on a POTUS OCONUS trip, to ease the inevitable jealousy), we returned to the hotel with plenty of time to have the book done early. We delivered it to the Ambassador's residence, where POTUS was staying, and even got a tour. It included a stop in the foyer where the Ambassador kept a record player, and we were recounted the story of POTUS dancing with the advance lead to a Prince song that morning. I was mesmerized by the sculptures on display, and by the marvelously large lawn on which POTUS had arrived via Marine One the previous night. We departed for the hotel, and discussions of dinner began (food is definitely a priority for me). As we were wrapping up emails and notifications for the next day, we realized that a meeting we hadn't been tracking had been added to the schedule without a briefing.

"POTUS can wing it," we were told.

That was not the answer we wanted to hear. Not providing a briefing would look like an omission rather than a vote of confidence at what the President could handle. In the eighth year of his presidency, Obama no doubt knew exactly what to say in virtually every meeting without reading the memos we provided for him. However, POTUS still read every page of those memos, and so they were prepared. Flabbergasted that we needed to explain this, we insisted that a memo be drafted and told our coworkers to go ahead to dinner without us.

While we waited for the memo to arrive, I went over the new briefing in my head. Had I missed something? Was this my fault? A year into my job, I'd stopped making small mistakes like not thoroughly reading the schedule. I'd gotten exponentially better at anticipating which events the President needed paper for and whom to expect it from. As I mentally walked through the process, I was relieved to realize that I hadn't missed it—I just hadn't been included in the discussion when the change was made.

Yet it stung. We had failed to deliver the President a complete book—my primary responsibility. It was a mistake I would have to own, even though I hadn't made it. That was tough.

Disappointed, we tried to figure out how to get the paper to POTUS, since he had already arrived back at the Ambassador's residence. The goal is always to disrupt POTUS and his personal time as little as possible. Therefore, the paper would tag along with the PDB, the Presidential Daily Brief, a product of the National Security Council (NSC), which was delivered by an NSC staffer first thing every morning—not to be confused with the book we pulled together every night. It wasn't ideal, but it was the best we could do. I had to shake off the frustration—we were barely halfway through the trip—and around ten p.m. we were finally free to eat.

The rest of the night didn't go any more smoothly, as we almost got mugged walking around town (thanks, Jon, for saving us!). But the final leg of the trip proved less eventful, by contrast. London is still my favorite city, and I got to deliver a book in a castle in Germany. I might not return to Saudi Arabia, but I survived and learned some valuable lessons.

As it turns out, there will always be more to learn.

November 2, 2016
My last trip. We had a jam-packed two days, with stops in Raleigh, a tour through Miami, and appearances in Jacksonville . . . all in less than thirty hours. Welcome to campaign season! (Though, to be honest, all our trips seemed to be this impossibly packed.)

I boarded the plane, preparing myself for the craziness that was about to descend. We took off at one p.m., meaning I only had two hours before memos started to pour in, and the number of stops on this trip meant I needed a serious game plan.

On autopilot at this point, I grabbed some boxes of presidential M&M's for our hotel staff and a few pieces of ordinary candy for myself. I had a feeling I was going to need the sugar rush soon. I took my seat at the table and spread materials out to start assembling an outline of the book. If the tabs were planned and organized ahead of time, it was easier to shove paper where it should go, especially when time was of the essence. I opened my computer and checked my emails, lining up colored pens to start my list. Color coding is *always* a good idea.

Shortly after takeoff, I got my first important email—but it wasn't one I expected. It was the kind of email that makes you pause. A staff member's father had died, and the funeral would be held that weekend. The President wanted to get a note to this staffer, but since we wouldn't return to DC before she left for the funeral, we needed to transmit a copy of the note back. This wasn't a normal email or scan.

It wasn't unusual for POTUS to handwrite notes, especially at times of hardship or big milestones. (My office even got one for the birthday card we gave him—a thank-you note for giving him a birthday card!) He knew that these notes meant a lot to people, and he happily took the time to write them.

Sure enough, I got a handwritten note at takeoff, in POTUS's beautiful script. I glanced over it quickly, for posterity's sake, and decided to put it back into the folder, lest a cup of coffee mistakenly go flying during some unexpected turbulence, or because of a staffer distractedly reading while pacing nearby. My instructions were clear: "trip [send] it back." Wi-Fi could be a little wonky, and it needed to be at the White House *now.* I walked over to the milaide (military aide) on duty, Rik Lawlor. Embarrassed that in my twenty-month tenure I'd never needed to trip something back (send something via secure communications on the plane), I asked him to show me how it's done.

Rik took me past POTUS's conference room, past the front entrance to the plane, and to a set of stairs I'd never noticed before. We ascended to a broad landing. Two members of the military sat at a desk in front of me, staring at computer monitors with what looked like an old-school radar system, displaying our plane flying over the states in slow motion. To my right were bunks where I was told the rotating pilots rested. One was indeed sleeping there! To my left was the cockpit, with a small desk just before the entrance.

Rik then introduced me to the man sitting at the communications desk. I handed over my cargo and told him where to trip it, explaining the importance and urgency of the situation. Not that anything the President needs to send back to the White House is unimportant, or that this man would for any reason delay its transmission, but I explained anyway. I peered over his shoulder as he put headphones on, as if I could discover how the process worked through observation alone.

Looking back at the men attending the two monitors, I tentatively asked, "What is that?" I wasn't sure if I was staring at something top secret that I shouldn't be asking about.

"That's tracking the strength of our Wi-Fi signal," one man explained.

Not so top secret.

At that point, Rik asked me if I wanted to meet the folks flying the plane—while they were flying it.

The crew was seated four deep: two pilots, with two additional military personnel in seats behind them. All I saw out the front window was clear blue sky. One of the guys in the back row waved silently at me as I mouthed "hi," and after another moment of gawking, I turned back around.

Mission accomplished, and then some. I headed downstairs to start my day of lasts on a day that had still held so many firsts for me.

- Last POTUS speech.
- Last AF1 sunset.
- Last AF1 beer. (Priorities.)

These trips were just a piece of my job. I am so proud to have served—to have been a small part of how government touches people's lives. I was fortunate to witness how the President can, and did, inspire people, and I was humbled by the opportunity to help make our country just a little bit better each day. Yes, I was sad to leave behind those unique opportunities and experiences when I walked out of the West Wing for the last time—the plane rides and motorcade travel, the privilege of being backstage while our president gave an impassioned speech, the satisfaction of being part of a historical administration. But what I miss most is what his presidency, and being a part of it, meant to me personally.

I had the good fortune to be included in a White House that employed and empowered young people. That provided them—me—an opportunity to experience a presidency up close. I know

I will not be the last young woman who discovers and revels in what an incredible privilege it is to serve. I am so thankful for all of those who helped me get there, from my amazing parents to my supportive office to the people I got to work and travel with who helped me grow and never let me take myself too seriously. I am a stronger, more confident person because of this adventure, ready to continue kicking ass and to ensure that the next generation of resilient women knows where they belong—in the White House.

Thanks, Obama.

JENNA BRAYTON

Title: Associate Director of Content and Operations
Office: Office of Digital Strategy
Age: 26
Date: March 20, 2015

Do what you can, with what you have, where you are.

I stood in the East Room of the White House—where the Civil Rights Act was signed and the foundation for the United Nations was laid. We had converted the historic room into the most amazing movie theater on the planet and were hosting almost one hundred children and young adults to watch student-made films. "If you don't stop and look around," Noah Gue, one of the filmmakers, said to the camera, channeling his best Ferris Bueller, "you're gonna miss it." The camera panned to a gorgeous shot of a rushing river hemmed with ice and snow. Noah, a native of Montana, made his film to spread awareness about the issues facing our environment. But Noah wasn't your average filmmaker. Noah was just six years old.

This was the White House Student Film Festival, an event mixing entertainment, government, and civic responsibility. Like Cannes or Sundance, its guests included many of Hollywood's brightest stars—Hilary Swank, Jake Johnson, and La La Anthony among them. The goal of the day was to inspire everyone to think about the meaning of service.

As I stood there—in the White House, on a literal red carpet—I finally understood how *I* could be the change I wished to see in the world.

★ ★ ★

The first time I remember hearing Barack Obama speak, I was about thirteen years old and I was with my mom at a mall in Illinois. This was long before Barack Obama was well known, back when he was just a state senator with, as he puts it, a funny name. When Obama was thinking about running for a seat in the U.S. Senate, he traveled around Illinois, talking to potential voters. My mom and I were out running errands when we saw him. We had just eaten lunch and I remember I was upset because my mom wouldn't let me get my ears double pierced, something I'd wanted for ages. The issue came up every time we were at the mall—Claire's was a conspicuous presence in suburban America back then. I was unhappy, but when I walked past a small group gathered to hear this state senator speaking, I stopped to listen.

There was something about him. He seemed genuine, authentic, and warm. He talked about duty to others. And he had, even then, an incredible way of captivating his audience.

I took note of him that day. And long after that speech at the mall, Barack Obama still had a profound effect on me. I remembered what he had said to us. And I began to talk to people about him. Barack Obama was a Harvard-educated lawyer. He could have accepted a job in any law firm in the country. But instead he moved to the South Side of Chicago to be a community organizer because he wanted to make people's lives better. And he ran for state office because he wanted to fight for the rights of those same people.

My life continued, and I never got that double piercing. But I did continue to think about Barack Obama. I put a few newspaper clippings about him up on my bulletin board next to some small blue-and-white Obama posters that I had hung behind my computer, right next to my pictures of Kate Middleton.

A few years later, in 2004, Obama gave the keynote speech at the Democratic National Convention (DNC)—the nominating convention of the Democratic Party. The party chose John Kerry as the presidential candidate that year, but to me, Obama's speech was the highlight. Watching it at home on TV, sitting on my pink carpet in my childhood bedroom, surrounded by those blue-and-white posters, I was once again moved by his words.

As he closed at the DNC, Obama talked about hope. "Do we participate in a politics of cynicism, or do we participate in a politics of hope?" he asked. "Hope in the face of difficulty, hope in the face of uncertainty, the audacity of hope." Listening to him that night, my fifteen-year-old self began to believe that maybe he was right—maybe ordinary people really could do extraordinary things. He made me think that if we all did our share, together we actually could build a fairer, more just, and more equitable world. I knew then that I wanted to be part of Obama's mission— I wanted to help build that world.

In the fall of 2006, I left home and headed to college. I briefly thought about studying art—I love how visual storytelling can reflect complicated, nuanced feelings about the world. Though the first course I registered for was an art class, I ultimately decided I was better with a pen than a brush. Barack Obama had inspired me to try to make a difference, but I had to do some searching to discover what that really meant for me. So I experimented with every mission-oriented class I could think of. I took classes in nuclear engineering to learn more about energy conservation and in psychology to discover how to help individuals; I was trying to figure out how to make this vague notion I had about improving the world just a little more real. I wasn't sure what I wanted, but I knew it should be something that allowed me to be heard, to stand up and fight for my values and make a tangible impact. And then I took a course in political science and started to understand how I could help shape the laws and policies of this country. Barack Obama had studied political science too, and as I sat in the first class, listening to the professor talk about the structure of our government, I felt like I had found my place.

Political science and the study of government offered me a chance to be useful to society and to help others in ways both big and small. For the first time, I saw how working in government might be an option for me. And I had the audacity to believe Barack Obama and his mission of change—and to believe in hope.

Fast-forward a few years to graduation. As I was leaving school—and panicking about what would come next—I started to think a bit about what I actually wanted to do with my newly minted political science degree. I loved political science, but how did I translate what I had learned in school into a job? At the time, I was a little jealous of my friends who had chosen majors like nursing or engineering—they had clear career paths in front of them, and mine seemed very messy. Who hired political scientists, anyway? How could I ever change the world? But the more I thought about what to do next, the more sure I became of the steps I would take. I certainly didn't know what it looked like to change the world—but I knew someone who had done just that. The answer I had been looking for came to me: I needed to work for Barack Obama.

Everyone thought that was a ridiculous plan—they wanted me to "be practical"—but I had made up my mind. And so I did everything I could think of to get an interview with him. I tweeted at his campaign basically nonstop. I called campaign headquarters. I did everything you shouldn't do when you're hoping to get hired. And when his campaign finally emailed me, asking me to come in and talk to them—probably just to stop the tweeting—I went all out. I painted my nails red, white, and blue. The day of the interview, I showed up with all the Obama paraphernalia I owned. I brought a ticket from the very first Obama rally I attended, just for good luck. I wore an Obama shirt under my suit jacket. I talked incessantly about how much I loved the man. And somehow it worked—I actually got hired. And that campaign job set me on a course that would one day lead me to stand in the East Room on a red carpet—it led me to a position working for Barack Obama at the White House.

★ ★ ★

I initially joined the very first White House digital team—known as the Office of Digital Strategy (ODS)—a team tasked with assisting President Obama in finding his voice online. We helped the

White House adapt to the new world of social media and digital communications. And it was while I was a member of ODS that I started work on the White House Student Film Festival.

In October 2013, President Obama issued a challenge to young people, grades K through 12, across America: tell us, using the medium of film, why technology is important to your education. Students responded to his question with nearly three thousand films. Sixteen of those films were selected for the festival, and the filmmakers were invited to present their works to Kal Penn, Bill Nye, Neil deGrasse Tyson, and of course, President Obama himself. Conan O'Brien also joined through a video call. The initiative stemmed from the idea that not only do young people understand what's going on in the world, they have points of view. They have passion and drive, they have boundless creativity. President Obama wanted to open the doors of the People's House to these kids and amplify their voices—after all, it's their world too.

A few months later, I was given the chance to help run the second (now annual) White House Student Film Festival. This was not part of my regular duties in ODS, but since joining the White House, I'd felt connected to the initiative. I loved the uniquely exhilarating energy of the young students who attended the festival. I loved that it was a chance for kids from all different backgrounds, with different perspectives, to use art as a tool to discuss something they felt was important to the American story. And it was a really cool opportunity for me because the film fest was changing a lot from the first year. Admittedly, I angled for the gig. I had asked my ODS teammate and friend Adam Garber a number of times to bring me on as cohost of the event. (Sometimes you just have to ask for what you want!) Adam was the genius behind the first film fest, and on its second iteration, he picked me to help him run it. When he asked me, I of course said yes—and right after that, I ran to the single-stall bathroom in the Eisenhower Executive Office Building and I cried a little, mostly tears of joy (it's okay to go to your crying place sometimes). I was thrilled, but I also knew I had my work cut out for me. Adam was putting a lot of faith in me.

Each year the film fest chose a theme. It was designed to help Americans think about and showcase things that were important to us as a nation. Adam and I, and two of our other Digital Strategy teammates and fellow film aficionados, Jillian Maryonovich, Hope Hall, and Thomas Kelley—TK for short—brainstormed. We spent many nights holed up in Hope, TK, and Adam's office, surrounded by cameras on every surface (they *were* the video team, after all) and sitting on the giant inflatable balls we used as chairs, kicking around ideas. The theme needed to reflect what we believed to be the core values of the Obama Administration. I thought about my first encounter with then state senator Obama in the mall. And I thought about his 2004 DNC speech, which discussed hope and fighting cynicism. He inspired so many young people like me. We wanted the film fest to do the same. Then the theme came to us, and it couldn't have been simpler: service. The core values that underscore a desire to serve—empathy, understanding, and kindness—were the perfect manifestation of our President. Plus, we wanted even our youngest citizens to think about how they could help their communities. We wanted kids to show us, in their own words, how they were making their communities and neighborhoods better. We called our theme "The Impact of Giving Back." Best of all, President Obama liked the idea!

With no time to waste, we got the ball rolling. The American Film Institute (AFI) had, for the second time, agreed to be our film fest partner. AFI is an organization that seeks to lift up, educate about, and preserve the history of filmmaking. The partnership with AFI was particularly meaningful because AFI was an idea born in the White House Rose Garden. In a 1965 speech, President Lyndon B. Johnson pushed for the creation of a film institute to preserve the heritage of motion pictures. He proclaimed, "Art is a nation's most precious heritage. For it is in our works of art that we reveal to ourselves, and to others, the inner vision which guides us as a nation. And where there is no vision, the people perish." With those words from our thirty-sixth president, AFI was born.

We started having conversations with our partners, which, in addition to AFI, included Participant Media. Participant Media sets itself apart from other film studios by focusing on elevating stories that have societal impact and that bring attention to issues of social concern. But these aren't the boring films your high school second-period sub might put on—this company makes certified hits. They're the brains behind some of the biggest blockbusters and award-season darlings of recent years, including a few of my favorites—Oscar-winning *Spotlight,* Oscar-nominated *The Post,* and *The Help.*

To kick off film submission season, we wanted the President to record a video that we would post online. This was a little tricky. Anytime the President gave his time to a project, it had to be signed off on by many layers of senior staff and coordinated with precision—literally down to the minute—by the scheduling team and the President's senior aides. Even a thirty-second film spot must be approved and then executed between meetings with dignitaries, security briefings, and speeches.

Once we had the go-ahead, we shot the announcement—quickly. "That's a wrap." President Obama smiled at the end of the spot. Since he was speaking to kids, he had the opportunity to be a little more casual and fun in the recording than usual. Suffice it to say, he was, and is, a true natural in front of the camera and barely needed any coaching.

With the announcement footage secured, Adam, as our Digital Team Video Director, edited the material, and in November, four months before the film fest, we went live. President Obama's video did the trick. Hundreds of submissions started rolling in. All we had to do was review them. All of them. *That* took some time.

Organizing the White House film festival was exactly what I wanted to be doing, but the work came in addition to my other responsibilities. To give ourselves a place to focus on the film fest, Adam, Jillian, Hope, and I commandeered a small space in a relatively secluded part of the EEOB, where we could gather to review the submissions after our usual long, taxing days. We took over part of the most unusual conference room in the White House—unlike the rest of the rooms, which were stately, historic, and elegant, this one had been converted into a high-tech space. It had green walls and Smart Boards and looked like it belonged in a Silicon Valley start-up.

Life in the White House is enormously busy, and there's rarely time to go out and get food, much less meals my mom (or anyone?) would approve of. Instead, for months, most film fest nights were capped with every sugar-based dinner imaginable in that little green-walled room. I regularly smuggled cake from the White House Navy Mess—where it was frequently someone or something's birthday—to the screening room to serve as my dinner. And when there wasn't cake, there were endless boxes of presidential M&M's, desk candy, and home-baked goods du jour brought in by colleagues who knew that sugar was responsible for 75 percent of our success. These "meals" weren't healthy, but they did help melt away the stress of a long day and were the perfect accompaniments to an evening of films. Sometimes you just have to eat the cake.

We were committed to reviewing every film that was submitted by the February 2 deadline—even the ones we got just minutes before they were due (and yes, we got *a lot* of films minutes before the deadline). The submissions came from all over the country. We even attracted international attention from a class halfway across the world in Azerbaijan! The films were multidimensional and thoughtful. Some of them had great plotlines that kept us guessing. Some featured impressive cinematography. They had narratives! And storytelling! Everything was original— original scores, original scripts, and original characters. I don't think I could have done that when I was a kid.

After months of deliberation, and after many late-night calls with AFI, we ended up picking fifteen films as Official Selections. In an ideal world, we'd screen all the submissions at the film fest, but it just wasn't possible. As a way to include as many students as we could, we featured some of the didn't-quite-make-the-cut selections on the White House YouTube channel. We wanted the young people to know that we, and President Obama, honored and appreciated their work.

With the selections down, we turned our attention to planning the actual event. I had never put on a film festival before, but there wasn't exactly time to sit around and study to become an expert. Instead, I learned everything on the go—how to set up and build an event for hundreds of people, how to manage competing stakeholders with different visions, how films are produced and video content is distributed on a large scale. As one part of execution, I was in charge of the guest list—students, celebrities, and everyone helping to produce the day. In total, including the crew, it came to about 150 people. To keep track of everyone and all their WAVEs—the identifying information Secret Service uses to vet someone before they walk through the White House gates—I made huge spreadsheets. The spreadsheets were important not only for keeping track of everyone but also in plotting out where they'd enter the White House complex. Students, celebrities, and crew had to enter via different gates at precise times. At the White House, you don't just WAVE someone in for the day—you WAVE them in at a *specific* time. If they don't get there on time, they can't enter. All of the people and all of their movements had to be choreographed precisely down to the minute. As I was getting ready for the event, I made a blueprint of the White House complex and laid it on the floor. Then I used Post-it notes to map all 150 individuals' entry and exit points.

Once the guest list was set, I asked the White House calligraphers to make some of our VIPs' invitations stenciled with their names. Even after many years working for President Obama, I still felt giddy when I opened a White House envelope on which my name was elegantly written in calligraphy. I was sure our guests would feel the same way.

★ ★ ★

Before we knew it, March 20, 2015, was upon us. We transformed the East Room into a movie theater. (The White House actually has a movie theater, but with seating for only about forty, it wasn't nearly big enough to host us.) We set up a stage, placed screens in front of it, and filled the floor with seats. We even turned the Blue Room and Red Room, state parlors typically used for formal receptions, into greenrooms for our celebrity attendees. We ran around finalizing the finishing touches. Near the students' entry into the building I laid out "tickets" to the film fest that the students could take and keep as mementos of their day. Jillian set up the step-and-repeat—a White House film fest–branded banner that students could stand in front of to take pictures—while Adam created the email chains we would use to coordinate our movements—down to the minute—and communicate all day. The White House Visitors Office, the team that helps execute personal White House events, was there too, helping us think about all the last-minute details and ensuring that the event went smoothly.

Right on schedule, at 12:30 p.m., the kids started to arrive. They were delighted to find that we had actually rolled out a red carpet in the White House East Wing! We invited E! News, who brought cameras and microphones, and La La Anthony, who showed up wearing a fabulous white suit and interviewed the kids as they walked down the red carpet toward our makeshift theater. The smiles on the faces of the students as they took selfies on the red carpet were unforgettable.

To garner additional attention for our work and shine a spotlight on the students, a number of big Hollywood names were invited. Along with the kids, the East Room was filled with stars like Hilary Swank, Jake Johnson, Michael Ealy, Amber Riley, and

Kal Penn. Steve McQueen and Bianca Stigter (who directed and produced *12 Years a Slave*, respectively) and Will Packer and his team from Will Packer Productions (whose studio has produced hits like *Think Like a Man* and *Girls Trip*) were there too. The President and CEO of the American Film Institute, Bob Gazzale, who was instrumental in putting the event together, joined them. Plus, Ken Howard and David White, the President and National Executive Director of the Screen Actors Guild–American Federation of Television and Radio Artists (SAG-AFTRA)—the union that represents most of Hollywood's actors and media personalities— were in attendance, as was Chad Boettcher, the Executive Vice President of Social Action and Advocacy at Participant Media.

After our VIPs walked the red carpet, the students could mingle with the experts in a special area we had set up. All the Hollywood celebrities, executives, and directors took their roles very seriously, wanting to make this the best possible event for the kids. With the same level of attention and professionalism they would bring to their own premieres, they chatted with and interviewed the students. I heard Hilary Swank talking to students about her career and the importance of jumping at opportunities. And I saw La La Anthony patiently and kindly talking to the students about building industry connections. They had so many questions for her about how to get jobs and how to get attention, especially when you don't have a platform, and she answered every one of them.

Once the kids settled into their seats, it was the moment we had all been waiting for. President Obama himself kicked off the event, welcoming the group to the White House with warmth, excitement, and statesmanship. Adam, Jillian, and I had been tracking his timeline and movements on our email chain—as staff, you always have to be ready for him—so we knew he was heading over to us before he got there. The moment he walked into our event . . . well, to say I was excited is a huge understatement. And then to see him up on the stage—the stage that we built!—introducing the film fest that we made from scratch felt like a huge achievement. He spoke for a few minutes about the importance of service, and he promised the kids that he was going to watch all of their films later. He couldn't stay for the whole event—it lasted about five hours—but I made a note to myself to make sure that we had the films ready for him. After all, as we knew, President Obama was true to his word. Especially when it came to kids.

Part of the reason the preceding few months had been so busy was because the film fest wasn't the only focus of the day. Early on, we knew that our event needed to have enduring impact. That's the amazing thing about every initiative that came out of President Obama's office—no single event hosted by the White House was just for the fun and glamour of it; each event had to be a launching pad for lasting, positive change. AFI had already agreed to match all the students participating in the film festival with an industry mentor, which was incredibly generous of them. So Adam, Jillian, Hope, and I worked with AFI and SAG-AFTRA to develop and implement a new program that we named A Call to Arts, with the aim of inspiring and supporting young artists of all backgrounds. After months of secret planning, late nights, and lots of coffee, we were finally able to publicly announce the program.

To support A Call to Arts, AFI and SAG-AFTRA asked their members to sign up to mentor students around the country in the field of their expertise. AFI and SAG-AFTRA agreed to collectively donate *one million hours* of mentorship to young artists!

President Obama announced A Call to Arts from the film fest stage. Listening to him talk about the program we had built filled me with pride. For me, it was one of those moments in life when everything just converged. There I was, standing in the White House, listening to the President talk about something I had accomplished. I was doing everything I wanted to be doing. I was working to help people. I was telling their stories. I am just an ordinary person, but on that day I really understood that we ordinary people can do the extraordinary.

After the President left the stage, we turned down the lights and it was time for the first surprise of the day. While he wasn't actually able to be there in person, JJ Abrams—who has directed films in the Star Wars, Star Trek, and Mission: Impossible franchises, just to name a few—filmed a segment welcoming the students. Some of the kids gasped audibly when he appeared on-screen. JJ spoke about how he had wanted to be a director from the time he was eleven (about the same age as a number of the kids in the room) and how they should chase their dreams, reminding them that he was living proof that they could do it. He also congratulated all the students on their great films. The kids were *beside* themselves. (Honestly, I sort of was too. I couldn't believe it was all finally happening.)

Then two-time Oscar winner Hilary Swank introduced the first set of films. She gave a remarkable speech—short but powerful. Hilary told the students how she grew up in poverty and felt like an outsider because her family didn't have a lot of money. But films and movies were her escape. "Art . . . it saved my life," she told the crowd. She concluded with a profound notion: "The most important person when it comes to defining and achieving success is you." She was speaking to the kids in the room, but that's great advice for anyone of any age.

Then the first film began. I was standing off to the side of the stage, but I was still pinching myself. I had already seen all the entries many times, but in that dark converted East Room, filled with the filmmakers themselves, they felt brand-new.

Six-year-old Noah Gue made a film that featured him bundled up in outdoor gear, in different climates, looking at the wild environment around him and pondering what could happen to our planet in the future if we don't take care of it in the present.

Julissa Perez, Shaun Besman, and Daniella Pereira—three high school students and best friends from Palm Beach County, Florida—created a film called *Give It All Away*. It was a slam poetry performance that addressed selflessness, radical kindness, and how we are born equipped to inspire others. It was beautifully shot and edited. They even composed the music themselves. Sitting there, watching them use their platform to speak up, I had tears in my eyes.

Desmond Bournes and Ajamu Austin from the South Side of Chicago made a film about using the tools at your disposal—including hip-hop—to overcome adversity. Desmond and Ajamu filmed their hip-hop video, which was about staying in school and pursuing an education, using more than one hundred male actors both from their school, Gary Comer College Prep, and from the Gary Comer Youth Center. It was empowering to witness passionate young men helping others to think differently about their circumstances.

Sprinkled throughout the film screenings were addresses by our Hollywood ambassadors:

- Kal Penn, a former White House staffer himself, got onstage to talk about why film matters to him. He is an actor, of course, but he also used to work in the Office of Public Engagement. He stepped away from acting for a period to dedicate himself to public service. This event, he told us, represented the perfect intersection of his life's work.
- Steve McQueen, director of *12 Years a Slave,* talked about how his journey to film came about because of his desire to make a social impact.
- Amber Riley, a lead actress in *Glee,* said she believed that you can use entertainment as a vehicle to talk about social issues, as well as issues of justice and opportunity. Films can change hearts and minds.
- Michael Ealy, an actor in *Think Like a Man,* discussed President Obama's campaign slogan—Hope—and how being in that room, with those inspiring young filmmakers, made him really hopeful for the next generation.

The overarching theme of the speeches, I found, was that entertainment is crucial in bringing together people from different backgrounds and beliefs. The film *12 Years a Slave* portrayed the true brutality of American slavery. *Glee* brought LGBTQ issues to the forefront of mainstream television. Movies take us out of our lives and drop us into the lives of others. Movies can make us more connected, more understanding, and more empathic. Movies make the world smaller and less scary. Whether they're about a kid struggling with devastating loss and a boat-borne tiger, or a shipwrecked alien who just wants to phone home, movies can bring us together and reveal fundamental truths about us. Sometimes the biggest impact we can have on society is through storytelling, and as the speakers emphasized, a passion for storytelling can start at any age. In fact, the voices and energy of young people often resonate the loudest.

At some point during the event, I stopped and looked around at everyone enjoying this thing we had created together. The students were laughing, and I was surprised to see that a few were even crying. I didn't have to wonder how they felt. I could see it in their faces. And I felt it myself. Already I had laughed and cried many times, but seeing these students so transfixed and happy—it was one of the most rewarding moments of my life.

Toward the end, Adam gave a short but sweet tribute to the film fest itself. He was usually a behind-the-scenes guy, so it was a lot of fun to see him onstage, talking about this thing that we had built. He thanked everyone for attending, and I felt an immense sense of accomplishment swell in me.

We had actually done it!

Pretty soon after the event was over, the students began to pack up. The next day was a big one—AFI and Participant had planned a series of educational programs so the students could sharpen their filmmaking skills and learn from the experts. Once they had headed out to rest up for day two, we began the second part of our day: evening tours of the West Wing to thank our celebrity participants for donating their time and talents to the festival. However, West Wing tours couldn't begin until the President wrapped up in the Oval Office around seven p.m. To pass the time, and because we were all starving at that point, we ordered some pizzas and crossed the White House complex, relocating to the Eisenhower Building next door for a small celebratory party.

As the clock hit seven, our tour began. Adam, Hope, Jillian, and I took Jake and Dan Johnson, Hilary Swank and some of her friends, La La Anthony, Amber Riley, and some of the AFI folks through the building. We worked in tandem, showing them around the West Wing. As staffers, we were able to bring family and friends on tours of the West Wing at night and on weekends, so this was something I had done before. But that night was certainly different. It's always a can't-believe-this-is-my-life moment to take someone around the West Wing, but with Hilary Swank, Jake Johnson, and La La Anthony in tow, it was really surreal.

Hilary Swank was especially interested in the history of each room. We showed them the Cabinet Room—the meeting space for the President and Secretaries of federal departments and agencies. While it's not always Cabinet meetings that take place in there, you can't use it unless the President is in attendance. We wandered down the hall and peeked into the Roosevelt Room, named after both President Theodore Roosevelt, who built the first West Wing, and his cousin, President Franklin Delano Roosevelt, who built the Oval Office as we know it today. Then we stepped outside to visit the Rose Garden. It's one of the most iconic and historic places in the West Wing complex, having hosted visitors, ceremonies, and presidential statements since its redesign during the Kennedy Administration. And we popped into the Press Briefing Room. We took a few photos in there, since it was the only space where photos were allowed, and I role-played the job of the press secretary with Hilary for a few minutes, jokingly asking her about the breaking news of the day. (In another life she'd have made a great White House Press Secretary!)

And last but not least, no West Wing tour is complete without a stop at the Oval Office. When we got there, President Obama had just finished working minutes before. I knew because the White House operations staff had sent me an email saying he was walking out and we were free to enter. During my tenure, I'd had the immense privilege to step inside on a few occasions, but each time it's awe-inspiring. It's arguably the most interesting and important room in the world. In reality, it's not that large or fancy. But there's something in the air that reminds you of the momentous power of the place, and I could tell that it was not lost on our guests that night.

During the tour, I chatted with Dan Johnson, one of Jake's guests. Dan was actually one of President Obama's students back when he was a professor at the University of Chicago. Dan and I share a similar worldview, and I think both of us would in part attribute that to the time we've spent around Barack Obama. He taught us how to organize—that if something needs to be done, we can lace up our shoes and do it ourselves. He taught us to look for pathways and to move forward—if a neighborhood needed a new community center, we should raise the money and build it. It didn't matter if we knew how to do that or not. If a White House film festival might inspire kids to build a better world, we should organize one. It didn't matter if it had never been done before. It was up to us to make it happen.

Walking around the West Wing with that group was unforgettable. There I was with a bunch of Hollywood celebrities, and they were asking *me* about *my* job, the place where *I* worked, and the president *I* worked for—and they thought *I* was the interesting one! Jake Johnson and Hilary Swank were curious about A Call to Arts. They both had been looking for the best way to put their resources to good use, and they were excited to participate in a program that I had helped build. Seriously? Pinch me!

That, to me, was really quite something.

Before I left for the evening, I strolled over to the East Wing to take one more peek at the movie theater we had created. I thought about the kids and special guests who had just occupied that space. My team and I didn't have a manual that showed us what to do or how to do it. Instead, we took initiative, and we adapted and evolved. When something didn't work, we looked for another route. We supported each other and found humor in the lighter moments. And we did that over and over again, hoping that eventually we'd be able to build something real.

Standing there, I had a flashback to President Obama's election. The day after he won, he spoke to a group of us at campaign headquarters. In a tiny, fluorescent-lit room, he addressed all the people, including me, who had worked tirelessly on his campaign. We were exhausted, but adrenaline charged the space. He said, "I try to picture myself when I was your age—and I first moved to Chicago at the age of twenty-five, and I had this big inkling about making a difference. I didn't really know how to do it. So when I come here and I look at all of you—it's not that you guys actually remind me of myself; it's the fact that you are so much better than I was. In so many ways: you're smarter, and you're better organized, and you're more effective."

He continued, "And so I'm absolutely confident that all of you are going to do just amazing things in your lives." At this point, President Obama began to cry, and so did I. To me, this is his legacy. He's inspired so many people to go out there and create change. And to some extent, that's what I hoped to do with the film fest. I wanted to lift up students' stories, but I also wanted to show them what they could do. I wanted to empower them, and I wanted them to see how much their voices matter.

Today, I'm still drawn to Barack Obama because his vision hasn't changed. He is still the same genuine, heartfelt man I first saw in that mall in Illinois. He still inspires me every morning to wake up and try to do something to help. He still believes in the power of ordinary people to work together to do the extraordinary. And so do I.

President Obama told young people they have to be the change they want to see in the world. I was always really proud of my position at the White House because I knew that every day I could help—and was helping—to make someone's life a little bit better. That's what service is.

Service isn't something we do occasionally, on the weekends, when we have time. Service is something we do daily. The story of America is, and has always been, a story about service. It's the story of ordinary people coming together to better their country, in whatever ways they can.

Service shows you that people aren't so different after all—we mostly want the same things for ourselves, for our families, and for our world. Service helps you connect with people, and it builds empathy and understanding. Service helps you, it helps your community, and it helps your country. *Do what you can, with what you have, where you are.* The kids who made those films knew in the core of their being this very basic truth: any one small thing can make an impact.

We forget this sometimes. But stories—and storytellers—remind us.

JAIMIE WOO

Title: Policy Analyst
Office: Office of the Vice President
Age: 24
Dates: November 16–19, 2015

There we were—just the two of us. Me and Joe Biden, sitting across from each other at a table in his cabin aboard Air Force Two. In front of me lay a large black three-ring binder bulging with cancer policy memos, notes, and reports covered in scribbles. In front of the Vice President lay a briefing memo from me, describing details of the cancer institute we were about to visit. I sat there silently as he read and highlighted portions of my writing. He looked up and asked me a question, and I produced some sort of answer. I realized that we were a mere foot apart. I had never been this close to the Vice President.

It was a whirlwind getting to that moment on Air Force Two, and the whirlwind didn't stop for the remaining year and a half I was on his staff.

★ ★ ★

When I joined the White House as a policy analyst in the Office of the Vice President (OVP), I was hired to provide support for more senior policy staffers. (This was, of course, after several rounds of interviews, followed by an unexpected phone-call offer, after which I jumped up and down in my kitchen and yelled "Oh my god!" thirty times to an empty apartment.) I quickly started working on a variety of issues, from LGBTQ policy to campaign finance reform, but I was the only staffer who covered health policy. So, during my first few weeks, I spent endless consecutive nights educating myself on my portfolio, or area of expertise, consuming information on the Affordable Care Act, Medicaid and Medicare, reproductive health, and other public health issues.

You might be wondering—how could a junior staffer be responsible for an entire portfolio for the Vice President? First, never underestimate a young woman. Second, we were a unique team within the Obama White House. OVP was one of the White House's eighteen departments, along with the Domestic Policy Council (DPC), the Office of Communications (Comms), and others. But within OVP itself, we had a mini policy office, a mini comms office, a mini everything—we were a microcosm of the White House. While the President might have had fifty-plus people in DPC working on every issue imaginable, the VP's office had about ten, each covering several policy areas. Mostly generalists, we relied heavily on experts from across the White House and federal agencies to supplement our knowledge.

The structure of our department made our team very close. Everyone knew one another, and meetings often took place in doorways, or as casual office drop-bys, or even in hallways for "walk and talks" (yes, those are real). We were also very different from the rest of the White House staff because our principal (gov-

ernment lingo for "the boss") was Joe Biden, not Barack Obama.
While the two obviously shared nearly identical policy agendas,
each had a distinct voice with his own perspective on issues and
his own managerial style. And while there were times when the
President's staff and our team didn't agree one hundred percent,
at the end of the day, we worked together as one White House.
We had the same mission: to serve our country with integrity, to
protect and strengthen the health and welfare of *all*, and to create
equal opportunities for Americans to achieve their dreams.

And to answer the question I get all the time . . . yes. There
were times I felt like I was living in an episode of *Veep*. Its depiction of randomly hilarious incidents that can only happen when
you're working at the highest level of government, combined
with fervent optimism and one-of-a-kind personalities, often hit
way too close to home. Once, a group of staffers, including me,
was told to hold movement (which basically means we were asked
to stop where we were and stand to the side) in the West Wing
due to the VP's impending arrival. As he walked by, other staffers
smiled and nodded, and many addressed him with "Hello, sir." I,
on the other hand, exclaimed with a disturbingly overeager smile,
"Hey, boss!" This is *not* how you address the Vice President of the
United States. It just sort of came out. I immediately turned an
unnatural shade of red, eyes wide. I was mortified. Even more so
when the VP winked at me.

Awkward greetings aside, we all worked extremely hard—we
served the Vice President of the United States, after all. The VP's
policy team might have been small, but we were mighty. When
Vice President Biden needed information on a particular policy
area for a speech, or when there was a significant update to an
issue, we hustled. When new events were added to his calendar at

the last minute, we stayed late. When he was traveling and those staffing him needed assistance, it was all hands on deck back in DC. Working as a junior staffer was an incredible opportunity for me to witness how the White House functioned (it definitely put shows like *The West Wing, House of Cards,* and *Scandal* into perspective), and it was inspiring to collaborate with knowledge-able, brilliant, and hardworking people on a daily basis (people like Leslie Knope *do* exist). My supervisor, Don Graves, despite having arguably the most demanding job on staff as Counselor to the Vice President, was a truly supportive and humble public servant. He never failed to encourage his staff to exchange ideas, speak up, and take credit for our work. If it weren't for Don, I wouldn't have been given the opportunity to work directly with Joe Biden, and I certainly never would have sat across from him aboard Air Force Two.

As a policy analyst, one of my most important responsibilities was putting together the Vice President's Daily Briefing Book. The briefing book was a binder, similar to Miranda Priestly's book in *The Devil Wears Prada*—it held essential information, was delivered each night, and was almost always with its owner. But its principal was much nicer than Miranda.

Each morning, after checking the VP's calendar, I'd determine the briefing materials he needed for the next day's events. I would then work with all the OVP departments, such as Speechwriting, Policy, and Scheduling, to gather memos, logistics, and research for the Vice President. If I overlooked an item, I could cause him to be underprepared for the day or leave him without expected

JAIMIE WOO ★ 201

answers. Yes, it's just a binder, but it's no small task, and so I became a binder expert. Needed an organized table of contents? I was the woman for the job. Couldn't find tabs? You could count on me. I was responsible for compiling, formatting, and copy-editing the material and then physically printing out the briefing book for delivery. Some days, this was a herculean task, as the VP had endless commitments and policy updates. Luckily, I alternated this daily compilation responsibility with another staffer, and our interns helped tremendously. Depending on where the VP was, I would either drop the binder off in the Situation Room for one of his military aides to pick up (casual, right?), or meet one of his aides to hand it off directly. It wasn't abnormal for me to be at the office past nine p.m.

Those twelve-hour days were tough—I canceled more plans than I kept. I ate at my desk most nights to stave off the hangriness. In the White House, that was the norm. Many of my colleagues, especially those who accompanied the VP on trips, regularly pulled twelve- to eighteen-hour days. We did what we had to do. But those late nights printing the VP's book were some of my favorites. It was fascinating to read about all of his upcoming events, some of which weren't public, and I learned so much about a variety of complex and pressing issues, from gun reform to retirement savings accounts. The hallways and offices were quiet; while people worked at the EEOB (Eisenhower Executive Office Building, the staff building right next to the actual White House) at all hours, it felt especially intimate being alone in the OVP wing. Sometimes I'd kick off my shoes and throw on some country music (controversial choice, I know). Other times I'd sit there in peace and soak up the silence after a hectic day. Completing a hefty briefing book was satisfying, particularly when I was able to get it out the door to the VP earlier than expected. There was something about being twenty-four and working at the White House until it was totally dark out; something about walking out of a nearly empty EEOB, down its grand Navy Steps, across West Exec, through the double doors of the West Wing, and into the Situation Room; something about being one hundred percent responsible for an item the Vice President of the United States relied on every single day.

A couple of months into my time on staff, the Vice President expressed increasing interest in finding solutions to fight cancer—specifically, cutting-edge treatments and therapies. This became my new policy portfolio. You could tell when the Vice President talked about cancer that it was more than an item on a checklist. It was personal. Shortly before I joined the team, his son Beau passed away after a grueling battle with one of the most serious types of cancer, a horrific brain cancer called glioblastoma multiforme (GBM). Because the White House is more than a workplace—it's a family—Beau's death devastated everyone, and that pain reverberated across the staff and across America. Witnessing the tragic aftermath influenced both how I understood the impact of policy and how I approached public service, and it illustrated just how interconnected the personal and political can become. The VP's desire to "end cancer as we know it" was sincere and emotional, but the power of his passion came from his knowing that he wasn't alone. Joe Biden knew that cancer touches millions of people, and so with his grief came resilience, urgency, and vision. He spoke with determination and led with a strength that made clear to everyone that Beau's death would not defeat him—it would make him stronger and empower him to help millions with his voice and his platform.

The Vice President sought to improve our health care system so that the government, as well as academic, nonprofit, and private sectors, might more efficiently organize their resources and collaborate in a patient-focused way. During his many trips to various hospitals and cancer centers with his son and his family, he found that too often, institutions lacked uniform software. Because the few vendors that serviced major health care providers had proprietary technology, it was nearly impossible for systems to "talk" to one another. This meant that hospital records, scans, and tests couldn't easily be transferred from one center to the next.

The Vice President wanted to fix this problem and facilitate a system that incentivized hospitals, health care providers, insurers, and technology platforms to work together. He would spend the remainder of his time as Vice President—and beyond—working to develop solutions. So when President Obama, during the 2016 State of the Union, asked Vice President Biden to become "Mission Control" and take the helm on a Cancer Moonshot, a reference to President John F. Kennedy's ambitious goal of putting a man on the moon, he was ready.

When the Cancer Moonshot actually took off, a set of qualified experts came together to form the VP's team. They developed a strategic plan to "dramatically accelerate efforts to prevent, diagnose, and treat cancer—to achieve a decade's worth of progress in five years." But early on, before the team was assembled, before the news coverage, and before the State of the Union, the VP wanted to learn the basics of cancer treatments to better inform his policy decisions. He sought to become an expert on the science behind the policy—the actual biology of how cancer therapies worked.

That's where Don and I came in. This is the story that hasn't been told.

★ ★ ★

The motorcade would depart from the White House at six a.m. Monday, whether you were there or not. So I traded in my Sunday-night Shakey Graves concert ticket for prep and a good night's sleep (not that it mattered—I was so excited I barely slept). The morning was cool and misty. I had never been to the White House that early, and the grounds were totally empty. As I walked through security, one of the Secret Service agents asked what had brought me to the office before dawn. I told him I was traveling on my first trip with the Vice President. He fist-bumped me. Those Secret Service men and women are the best.

I got to my office about forty-five minutes before I needed to, just to make sure I had all the necessary documents printed (I'd experienced too many broken-printer emergencies in the past). My office mate, who would also be on this trip, had a coffeemaker and generously brewed a pot. I owe so many of my alert and happy mornings to her.

We made our way down to West Exec to meet the more than ten colleagues who would be assisting the VP for various events. After we piled into the staff van, the motorcade took off to Joint Base Andrews. Let me tell you, riding in the motorcade is not for the faint of heart. All the huge bulletproof vans swerve side to side, neon lights flash and sirens blare, and the Secret Service drivers speed up and slow down randomly, all for security purposes. Nate Rawlings, one of the VP's speechwriters, once told me that during his interview process, he was asked if he got carsick—a legitimate question, considering how often he found himself typing up revised talking points and rewriting speech sections in the back of a moving vehicle. Nate always carried a portable printer in his backpack, and he had to pull it out to reprint remarks too many times to count. He also carried a three-hole punch to insert new remarks into the VP's briefing book (you know, the one I made). There was a running joke among the team, because even after all our work, the Vice President might end up improvising onstage. And for him, it always worked. A talented storyteller, the Vice President could always make his point without a script—his authenticity never failed to draw an audience in.

My office mate quickly became my travel buddy. Because it was her second trip, I looked to her for pointers on what to bring and how best to support the VP. I unfortunately didn't follow her advice on the former—though every piece of my research was accessible on the work laptop I had with me, I made the mistake of lugging all my paper notes in several gigantic binders. As the organizer of the VP's Daily Briefing Book, I became obsessed with binders—they managed my life. When I boarded the plane that day, I dragged my duffel bag; a large shoulder bag stuffed with binders; my winter coat, a blazer, heels, and flats; and my laptop, while I clutched both my personal iPhone and work BlackBerry. I *screamed* newbie.

This was a trip of many firsts: not only was it my first trip staffing the VP, but it was also my first-ever visit to California. I had never been to the West Coast, and what better way than to roll in on Air Force Two? As I climbed aboard the plane from the runway, I found that each seat had a name tag (I still have mine!).

The seats were assigned in order of seniority. As a junior staffer, I sat with a few other policy staff in the back and with the VP's trip director, Sam Myers, one of the most-well-known figures in the White House. He had been with the Vice President since the beginning of the Administration.

The flight attendants took great care of us—often checking in and offering snacks and warm towels—and the food on this plane was delicious (a sentence I'd never thought I'd write). Food is served on Air Force Two whenever you fly during mealtime, and I took advantage of that. (Of course, because we're public servants, they later send us a bill for our food. Literally no such thing as a free lunch.) Pro tip I learned from travel veterans: Given how utterly busy things get on these trips, you never know when your next meal or bathroom break will come along, so always eat and go to the restroom when you can. And don't forget to drink water. Coffee doesn't count.

Before this trip, I had never met with the Vice President one on one. In my previous briefings with him in his West Wing office, other staff or external folks were present. But that day was different. After we reached an appropriate altitude, Don walked back to me and said, "Boss wants to see you."

"Okay," I responded as I started to tremble, scrambling to change into my heels and gather that hefty, felt-like-it-weighed-thirty-pounds binder. I glanced at my plane neighbor, who said, "It's go time. Good luck." I walked up to the front, where senior staff sat, and paused to wait for Don, whom I fully expected to join me. He looked up at me from his laptop and said, "He asked just for you."

Oh God.

I apprehensively walked around the corner into his suite. "Hi,

Mr. Vice President." He looked up and motioned me to come over and sit down. It was very surreal. I kept thinking, *Is this actually happening?* I sat down in front of him as he flipped through a thick binder I had prepared, filled with information about cancer. I remember watching him take notes in the margins of my memos as I answered questions. To be honest, I can't remember much else. I must have blacked out from sheer shock. But I do remember how intently he looked at me when I spoke—his piercing blue eyes making contact with mine showed me that he was genuinely interested in what I had to say and took in every word. Duh, right? No wonder he was Vice President. He was so good at having a real conversation, and this was something that startled me. When I was a Joe Biden spectator from afar, I witnessed him speaking to large crowds with such charisma. As a natural public speaker and beloved leader, he exuded awe and respect. Now that I was up close, away from the rope lines and flashing cameras, it was clear that he was also a normal human being. He was someone who cared deeply about curing cancer and someone who sincerely wanted to learn. The VP's personal physician, Kevin O'Connor, affectionately known as Doc, later walked in to listen and offer insight. He had been with the VP throughout Beau's treatments, and supplemented our conversation with his own scientific and medical knowledge.

After my terrifying, amazing briefing with the Vice President, I was able to relax until we landed. I watched *San Andreas*—you know, the film with the Rock about a huge earthquake that totally destroys California? Yeah, that movie—on my first trip to CA. The rest of the staff teased me as I gasped and shrieked throughout.

★ ★ ★

After deboarding the plane, we piled into the second motorcade of the day, en route to our first cancer center. I'm sure we created quite a few headaches for LA drivers, as we shut down large stretches of highways and streets, but I also caught a glimpse of a few surprised faces and people desperately hurrying to snap photos. As we approached our destination, my heart started thumping. I needed to be ready. Things move very quickly when you're on the ground, and if you aren't paying attention, you'll get left behind. During prior VP events I'd staffed, I purposely hung back, kept my eye on Don so I knew where to go, and tried not to get in anyone's way. But this trip would be different.

The scheduling and advance team is incredible—they plan every single pathway prior to the VP's visit. An "advance" team basically gets to a location a few days (or weeks for international trips) in advance to scope out the place and report back on the locale's blueprint, exit paths, design, etc. They develop a step-by-step schedule and list of instructions, down to which elevator the VP will take and who will be in that elevator. The VP and his core staff, like Don and Secret Service, would take him where he needed to go. Remaining staff would follow; perhaps they'd take the stairs when there was only one elevator. While I attended some of these organizing meetings to get a better sense of the trip, you can never know exactly how things will play out until you get there.

It felt like time was moving in fast-forward. Because I was in one of the staff vans toward the end of the motorcade, by the time I got out and made it to the entrance, the VP was already in the building. I picked up my pace and scurried inside, only to see him stepping into the elevator that would lead him to a conference room where he'd meet with the research team I had briefed

him on. And where was I? Near the back of the pack, downstairs with the rest of the staff who weren't involved with this part of the trip. I had all my stuff with me, and I'm thinking, *Okay, now what do I do? Should I be up there?* My colleague, Greg Schultz, one of the most uplifting people I've met ever, and one of the VP's closest senior advisors, looked at me, smiled, and said, "Jaimie, this is all you. You gotta get up there! This is your trip. Go!"

I looked at him wildly and thought, *Oh, crap.* I frantically searched for a stairwell. As I ran up the stairs two at a time—in heels, no less—all I could think was *Come on, Jaimie. Enough. Enough doubting yourself. This IS your trip. This is why you're here.* For fear of giving myself too much credit, for fear that it was inappropriate to accompany the Vice President in his meeting because no one had told me to, and for fear of doing something wrong because of insecurity, uncertainty, and intimidation, I had lost sight of my purpose: to support the Vice President. *Pull it together, woman,* I told myself.

Out of breath and flushed, I finally reached the floor where the meeting was taking place. Outside stood the VP's bodyman, or primary bodyguard, John Flynn, known to all staff as Flynn, who looked at me with a warm smile and said, "They're right through there, Jaimie." How was it that everyone had faith in me but me?

I pulled open the doors and walked through with huge binders in my arms and an oversized bag holding more binders over my shoulder. Heads turned. "Sorry for the delay," I murmured. The VP looked at me reassuringly. They had already started the meeting, but he made it a point to acknowledge my presence by introducing me as someone who worked on his cancer portfolio. I got smiles and nods as I quickly sat near the end of the conference table. One of the doctors resumed his presentation, a PowerPoint

projected on the wall. As I took copious notes, I noticed that the binder I had prepared for the VP, the same one that had been in front of him on Air Force Two, was on the table in front of him again. He was skimming through my memos. Stomach flip.

At these early stages of his yet-to-be-named Cancer Moonshot, the Vice President wished to be more educated about the scientific discoveries that would inform his policy making. This particular meeting helped move the needle; it focused on the center's exploration of several developing treatments, such as immunotherapy, which harnessed the body's own immune system to fight cancer cells, and virotherapy, which can refer to the modification of viral cells so that they attack and kill cancer cells. While many medical institutions practiced these therapies, this research center had made strides that were of specific interest to the Vice President.

After the presentation, we walked downstairs and the doctor's team gave us a tour of his research facilities. As we passed doctors and staff, I saw dropped jaws and wide eyes. This trip was an OTR, or "off the record," which means that the press and general public did not know about the VP's visit. Some trips are deemed OTRs because they're for internal meetings, and others because they allow a lot of flexibility—while a few key people at a destination may know the VP is arriving, our staff can avoid large crowds and unexpected visitors. You better believe if folks knew, we'd be met with camera crews galore, and the VP wanted to avoid disrupting the center's daily functions.

I probably could have stayed close to the Vice President, but I chose to keep a bit of distance between us. This was partially because Don had everything under control, but also because I

was carrying so many things and looked a little ridiculous. . . . I didn't want to be captured in any of the photos. I kept setting my bag down because it was so heavy, wanting to kick myself for not packing light. Luckily, David Lienemann, the VP's photographer, kept me company between shots, so I didn't look too odd hanging back alone.

Staffing the VP in California was a high point I'll never forget. In less than twenty-four hours, I'd advised the VP directly, participated in the organized chaos of VP travel, and learned more about myself and about overcoming obstacles and insecurities than I had in the entire previous year. I truly didn't think it was possible to top it. But I was wrong.

Our next stop was Houston, Texas, my hometown, where the VP would not only meet with several oncologists and medical experts but would also meet my parents. He made it a point to try to greet his staff's family members whenever he visited cities they lived in. It was a wonderful gesture that meant a lot to the whole OVP team.

When we landed, some of the staff, including myself, peeled off from the motorcade as the VP headed to a separate event. Consequently, I was able to settle into my hotel room and welcome my parents. Upon the VP's arrival, the plan was for him to take photos with hotel management, a token of appreciation for their accommodation, and then pose for photos with me and my parents. My folks were anxious, and so was I. We waited for him on the top floor of a banquet hall where we could oversee downtown Houston—we were even able to watch the motorcade roll in, flashing lights and all. A look of shock spread across my mother's face when I told her that's how I got around town too.

I could hear the Vice President's voice before I could see him; he was on his cell phone and paused to hang up before turning the corner. As he approached, he saw two hotel staff members waiting for him by the photographer, but as he turned to them, he caught sight of me with my parents. He broke into a huge grin. I heard him say to the hotel staff, "Listen, I'm absolutely going to visit with you both in a second, but I just need to say hello to these wonderful people first. . . ."

My mom was speechless. She had the biggest, goofiest smile on her face. "How are you doing?" the VP asked. She tried to answer, but no sound came out. She just kept nodding vigorously and smiling and laughing. He clutched her hands the entire time. It was pretty adorable. Meanwhile, my dad, the chatterbox he is, couldn't stop talking and thanking him, likely out of nervousness: "Thank you for meeting us. You are such an inspiration. Thank you for all that you do. Thank you for meeting us. We are so proud of Jaimie. Your work on cancer is so important. Thank you for meeting us." I blushed, chuckling perhaps a little too loudly. It's probably not normal to black out from sheer happiness whenever you talk to your boss, but it's normal around here. I don't remember exactly what the Vice President said, but I do recall him saying I was doing a great job. He shared an anecdote about how children are a reflection of their parents and how we should be extra proud when they "turn out even better than us." I think he was referring to me. Whatever he said made my parents extremely happy. It was a surreal and beautiful moment, one that I will truly never forget.

It only hit me later how pivotal this moment was in my professional career and, beyond that, in my relationship with my parents. As Chinese immigrants, their experiences growing up couldn't have been more different from mine. My mom, for instance, struggled through the Cultural Revolution during Mao Zedong's communist rule. While her sister was forced to tend to fields in the countryside, my mother was instructed to work in a factory. Nearly everyone thought getting an education was a waste—upward mobility was not an option, and educators were persecuted. But my mother's father believed that education was of the highest importance, a common theme among Chinese families, and encouraged my mother to find a way to stay in school. So as a young teenager, she tracked down various government officials to pitch switching her position with a school attendee's. Her perseverance made her successful (and I like to think she gave me my knack for election door-knocking many years later). Although universities were closed during the Cultural Revolution, she attended a medical training school for two years and later worked as a doctor in a countryside clinic.

My mother embodies the American Dream. She worked extremely hard and was one of a small group of students who had a chance to come to America when the Cultural Revolution ended. After she was accepted to the University of Houston, she moved here with nothing but determination and a few words of English. With grit and strength, she earned her PhD. Like her dad, my mom deemed education the highest priority and the ultimate measure of success—it allowed her to provide for her family, escape turmoil in China, and earn the respect of her colleagues and friends in the States. She had hoped I would follow in her footsteps and become a doctor, but that was her dream, not mine.

My dad, similarly, followed a preprofessional path. He studied engineering, earned his MBA in night school shortly after I was born, and worked in the theme park industry as an electrical engineer for much of my life (which made for great birthday parties—thanks, Six Flags and Walt Disney World!). Because he grew up in Canada after relocating as an infant from China, he assimilated into Western culture at an earlier age than my mother. While this cultural difference often caused a rift between my parents, my father too felt that education was the path to success, and so, like my mom, he encouraged me to consider law or business school.

Both of my parents chose one straight path, and they stuck to it. My path hasn't exactly been straight—it's been full of crossroads, U-turns, and blockades. The cultural divide between me and my parents often put a strain on our relationship, one that was exacerbated by my career choices. They worried that a low-paying profession in public service wouldn't provide for me financially, and they were uncomfortable with a field they knew little about. School was the ultimate measure of success, and I hadn't gotten a PhD yet. . . .

But something changed after my parents' visit with the Vice President. While they didn't fully understand what I did on a daily basis or have any connections to the political world, meeting the Vice President of the United States was something concrete, something understandably important, and something spectacular. There was a moment of recognition of what I was capable of—recognition I rarely received—and an unspoken acknowledgment that despite their reservations, I'd gotten here of my own accord. My path might not have made sense to them, but I forged it myself, and it led me to accomplishments they could never have imagined.

★ ★ ★

While the VP showered me with praise to my parents (as he would often do with his staff), I can honestly say it's not something I regularly gave myself. When you're surrounded by some of the smartest, most driven people in the country, working with brilliant minds who seem to achieve things with ease, it's not unusual to get imposter syndrome, a feeling of not belonging with those around you. My colleagues had years of experience and expertise. As a young Chinese American woman, I didn't see many people who looked like me in politics. So how had I gotten here? Did I belong? Had they made a mistake?

There is a natural fear of being unable to live up to what's expected of you, and it took me a long while to get to this realization: You are not randomly here. The work you've put in and the experiences you've had have led you to where you are, and you were chosen for a reason. You might not know that exact reason, or even believe it, but that doesn't mean it isn't true.

On the VP's developing cancer initiative, for example, I might not have had extensive expertise, but in the beginning stages, as we were building up our ranks, I demonstrated that I was willing to work really hard. And there is something to be said about just working really hard. I did what was asked of me, and then I did more. I stayed late. I asked questions when I didn't understand. By letting my hard work speak for itself, I was relied on and then given further opportunities. But perseverance under pressure often comes with no praise—it's the nature of government service—and that can be difficult. It took months to finally learn that success was rewarded with more work, and more work meant there was trust and an understanding of a job well done.

As my responsibilities increased, I did my best to stay humble. One of the first lessons I learned at the White House had actually been years prior, as a summer intern in the Office of Management and Administration. The office's mantra was "No task is too small." When you're working for a greater mission and a greater purpose, these words are so true. The whole operation would crumble without people at every level of service. Whether you're an intern making copies or a senior staffer advising the President directly, you are a part of something bigger than yourself. It is never about you; it's about your shared mission.

So my own mantra? Hustle, work hard, and stay humble.

That being said, despite the importance of humility, every once in a while, when things got tough, I thought of my badass moments. Like the time Vice President Biden called me on my cell phone. It went something like this:

I'm home watching a movie with my friend when my Black-Berry's ringtone interrupts our focus. It's about ten p.m. I look at my phone. "Unknown," it reads.

"Hello, this is Jaimie."

"Hi, Jaimie. It's Joe."

Pause.

I look at my friend with wide eyes.

Longer pause.

"Oh, hi, Mr. Vice President!"

My friend's jaw drops. I leap up and start pacing around the room.

"I'm reading this memo you wrote about the GBM event I have tomorrow. It's really good, thank you."

The VP then went on to ask a couple of questions. I stumbled through getting my laptop out of my bag, in hopes of transcribing his exact words so I wouldn't miss a thing. Luckily, I was able to provide him some clarity.

After we hung up, I called my best friend, Emma. Then I called my mom.

That was a day I'll never forget. That was a day that I held in my pocket for the hard days.

After I said goodbye to my parents following our group photo with the Vice President, exhaustion hit me like a train. I fell asleep replaying the image of my parents meeting the VP over and over again. I woke up feeling rejuvenated, ready to join Don in the Vice President's hotel suite, where we would hear from more researchers and doctors on their institutions' cancer work. The VP greeted me upon my arrival and said how much he had enjoyed meeting my parents. I smiled sheepishly and said, "They were so appreciative of you meeting them—thank you."

As we settled around the conference table, I grabbed a couple of scones from the center console, where a large array of breakfast items sat (remember: eat when you can!). As the meeting started, I realized I was the only person digging in. There I was, chewing awkwardly, as everyone talked about the horrors of cancer with empty plates in front of them. Just perfect.

Peering around the table, I also realized I was the only woman present. It was a stark reminder that there are still not enough women in STEM fields, and similarly, in politics.

The Obama White House broke records when it came to hiring people of color, women, members of the LGBTQ community, and people with disabilities. The President placed people from traditionally marginalized populations in senior positions, and the Administration made it a priority to consider diversity in nearly every situation, whether it was hiring new staff, searching for speakers to visit the White House, or crafting events.

But improvements can always be made. As diverse as the Obama White House was, few women looked like me in OVP. It wasn't unusual for me to walk into a room and see no other women of color, which contributed to my imposter syndrome. One of the most prominent Asian American Pacific Islander (AAPI) women staffers was Kathy Chung, the Vice President's assistant, who sat immediately outside the VP's West Wing office. She was the VP's right-hand woman, and it was incredibly meaningful for me to see someone who looked like me in a senior leadership position at the White House. My hope is that more AAPI women consider politics as a career choice, and their families support them. My hope is that one day, we can change representation in politics so that everyone feels as though they belong.

The remainder of my trip was as much of a whirlwind as the start—after Houston, we continued on to events the VP had in other cities. The exhilaration continued back in DC. Over the course of the next few months, through meetings with various White House departments, federal agencies, and interested stakeholders, the Cancer Moonshot was slowly turning into a reality. I continued to provide the Vice President with research and participated in meetings he had with technology companies, business leaders, and other academic institutions. But as we inched closer to the State of the Union (SOTU), the VP was moving beyond the scientific and biological nature of specific cancer treatments—he was now exploring the health care system as a whole, thinking through solutions to the problems he and his family faced when Beau was undergoing treatments.

It was around this time, shortly after the President's SOTU address, when Don pulled me aside with a proposal that would change the rest of my time in OVP. He asked if I would be interested in joining the Violence Against Women (VAW) team, a subset of the Domestic Policy team. Combating violence against women was a huge priority for the VP (and still is), and so unlike most other policy issues, VAW-related events and policy issues went through the Vice President's Office.

I had a lot of thoughts and feelings, some of which I'm not proud of. By moving to a team whose supervisor reported to Don, was I being demoted? Did Don think I was incapable of being a part of the newly developed cancer team? Had I done something wrong? I was finally getting in my groove in my current role, and now I would have to start over. What would it be like working with this new team—would we get along? It took me a while to view this change as the new and exciting opportunity it was and not a setback. When I was able to simply shift my perspective and trust in the fact that I was an important asset to OVP and that Don wanted what was best for me, I couldn't wait to get started.

After all, I was most interested in and passionate about working on issues related to violence against women. When I first joined OVP, I had expressed this interest to Don and, as a result, had been able to sit in on VAW team meetings and assist with smaller projects. The sole reason I'd left my former job as a grassroots organizer on economic justice was to pursue work on women's issues and, more specifically, bystander awareness and sexual assault prevention. Now I had the chance to do so for the Vice President of the United States, Joe Biden, who had authored the Violence Against Women Act, a landmark piece of legislation that transformed the legal system to be more victim-centered and abolished the notion that domestic violence was a "family issue." Sign. Me. Up.

Working on those issues would change my life. It would introduce me to the strongest, most inspiring and courageous women I had ever known, teach me the true meaning of teamwork and humility, challenge me beyond belief, and leave me with stories that still make me double over in laughter after a hard day. And while I stayed incredibly busy with my new portfolio, as a veteran of cancer policy and knower of all things, thanks to my briefing book duties, I was still able to pop my head in on cancer events and planning meetings. How lucky was I to work on two of Vice President Biden's most important legacy issues?

A mentor of mine, Lacy Kline, who worked as the White House Internship Program Director during my OVP tenure, gave me an important piece of advice after I left the White House. As I considered what my next career steps would be, she told me, "What we went through, what we did, it was one of a kind. No matter what, no job will ever be exactly the same. Even if you went back and worked for Joe Biden now, it wouldn't be the same. And that's the beauty of it. Accept that and let it go. Find the next greatest adventure."

I think about Lacy's advice often, especially as I reflect on my White House journey. My work there was more than a couple of lines on my résumé; it was a formative period of my life, with stretches of both pride and disappointment. Did I yell in excitement and jump up and down after the VP called my cell phone? Yes. Did I feel super cool and important walking into the Situation Room most evenings? Definitely yes. But would I have done some things differently? Of course. I made mistakes—I'm the first to admit it. I once made an intern cry. I let my ego get the best of me. But making mistakes is a part of being in your twenties, right? Hell, it's a part of every decade of your life. It might be easy to think, *You were so young, so naive. You should have been more self-aware about X, Y, Z.* But the ironic thing is that a few years from now, I know I'll think the exact same thing about this moment right here, right now.

So what's my solution? To live in every single moment, to cherish and enjoy all my badass and beautiful experiences, and to accept that while I may not have all the answers, I can still enjoy and learn from my journey. My contributions will matter.

Nothing will ever compare to the unbelievable experience of working for Vice President Joe Biden during the Obama Administration, but I'm not worried. Because for me, and for every young woman out there, the next greatest adventure is waiting. We just have to go for it.

And next time, maybe I'll leave the huge binders at home.

NOEMIE C. LEVY

Title: Policy Assistant
Office: Domestic Policy Council
Age: 24
Date: October 1, 2014

The most memorable day I had at the White House wasn't in the White House at all. It wasn't even in Washington. It was actually in Brooklyn. That might sound surprising, but let me explain.

I had a lot of memorable moments working for President Obama. I remember the first time I heard my words in one of his speeches. It was just one sentence. The President was speaking about community service, and I had inserted a small amount of data into his remarks. I felt chills as I listened to him share the numbers I had researched and read the phrase I had written.

I remember the warm glow of lights reflecting off the gold woven curtains lining the walls of the East Room, giving the whole space a surreal, sun-drenched quality. I remember rushing in my favorite blue heels on the soft red carpet that lines the ground floor of the White House, briefing VIPs—from Fortune 500 CEOs to philanthropists—on the meetings they were about to have with our Commander in Chief. I remember sitting in the

Situation Room, presenting my work, and wondering how all the moments of my life could have possibly added up to get me there.

There were lighter moments too, like my first White House Hanukkah party. It's a beautiful party that the First Family hosts every year for prominent members of the Jewish community, including Jewish members of Congress and senior agency staff. Every once in a while, Jewish White House staffers score an invitation. The first time I went, I pinched myself as I stood with my friend Molly Dillon. We conducted the nerdiest possible version of "celeb-spotting," peeking from behind a doorway at Justice Ruth Bader Ginsburg, who stood in the food line, casually assessing the same latkes and brisket that sat on our plates.

Suffice it to say, many days working for the White House were unforgettable. But that day—the one in Brooklyn—was different. There was no glamorous reception, no rousing speech, no boisterous press conference. I spent the day hundreds of miles away, in Williamsburg, Brooklyn, in a tiny conference room full of strangers. But it was the most important thing I have ever done. On that day, I remembered why I'd first come to work for President Obama.

There were two major life events that brought me to the White House. There was the biggest challenge of my childhood: emigrating from my home in Paris, France, to the United States. My parents are Jews who immigrated to France from Morocco, but France is one of many countries that haven't always honored their Jewish communities—and the pain of that history was something they were often reminded of, even in daily, small ways. They

wanted to live in a place they were proud of, where they really felt like they could inhabit their cultural and religious identities freely. They found that in America.

At first, though, life in the United States was tough. I didn't speak a word of English and spent days in school in a confused haze. And learning English wasn't even the hardest part. A language can be learned, but social cues and expectations are a lot harder for a kid to pick up. For years, I struggled to fit in. I couldn't relate to my American peers and their American lives. I ate different food, watched different films, and read different books. I loved wearing patterned skirts, white-collared shirts, and ballet slippers—not exactly in style for South Florida tweens in the mid-nineties. It would be years before I felt a part of American culture.

But I found that even when America didn't make sense to me, science did. Science truly is a universal language; its principles extend beyond the boundaries of any one country. Therefore, in school I always gravitated toward science and math. They were a part of my identity before America fully was. I dreamed of becoming a doctor, like my mother. I wanted to sit with people, hear about their problems, and apply science to find a clear solution.

To my surprise, as the years in college went by, I realized I wanted more. I didn't want to be hunched over a lab bench, staring into a microscope. And no matter how fulfilling medicine seemed, I didn't want my impact to be on just one patient at a time. By the end of my sophomore year, I wanted to make a difference on a much bigger scale, and that's when I started thinking about working for the government.

Which brings me to the second huge thing that changed my trajectory. On Tuesday, November 4, 2008, Barack Obama was elected as our nation's first Black president. And just a few

months into his presidency, on April 21, 2009, President Obama signed into law the Edward M. Kennedy Serve America Act.

★ ★ ★

The Edward M. Kennedy Serve America Act was a landmark law that helped find smart solutions to address our nation's most pressing social problems—things like homelessness, unemployment, and inadequate access to health care and education. One important impact of the law is that it created the Social Innovation Fund, or SIF. Its goal was to find new ways to solve old problems. In that spirit, the President also launched a brand-new office, called the White House Office of Social Innovation and Civic Participation. (I know it's a mouthful, but the White House has so many offices, their names need to get pretty specific!)

I was sitting in the library at Rice University when I first read about the SIF, browsing the web while procrastinating on studying for a neuroscience class. I was moved by the idea that there was a group of people in the White House dedicated to inventing new methods to fix age-old social problems and create affordable housing, decent jobs, and good health care and education for all. The office was about promoting new kinds of partnerships—ones that involve businesses and foundations—recognizing that the government can't possibly solve these deeply complex problems alone.

Just a few months in the White House, and already President Obama was finding novel approaches to problem-solving. "*This,*" I remember thinking. "*This* is where I want to work after I graduate." But how could I get there?

I started by conducting countless hours of research, and

learned everything I could about the White House Office of Social Innovation and Civic Participation. I studied the organizations that received money from the Social Innovation Fund. Some created jobs for individuals who have been homeless or incarcerated—either of which can be a huge barrier to finding work. Others were improving health care for people living with HIV/AIDS.

My research was just the beginning. I applied for an internship at the White House, making it clear that I wanted to work in the Office of Social Innovation and Civic Participation. A few months later, I got a call from a young staffer in that office who wanted to interview me for the role. When she told me she wanted to hire me, I didn't think it was real.

But it *was* real. After several weeks of nervously refreshing my in-box every few minutes, I received an email. I was invited to start my internship. I had two weeks to move to Washington, DC.

I've always worked hard in school, but I worked harder than ever as a White House intern. It was not unusual for me to work from eight a.m. to ten p.m. or to come in on weekends. I started drinking coffee, which not only powered me through the long days and nights but also gave me an excuse to get a little fresh air on my afternoon runs to Swing's Coffee, a favorite spot among staffers. It would have been nice if someone told me when I was a teen that having a job is *much* harder than going to school—I was constantly getting assignments that needed to be done *immediately*. I managed the schedule of the office's director and planned events. I drafted memos that would work their way up the chain from the director of my office to his boss, the Director of the Domestic Policy Council, and sometimes to *her* boss, the President of the United States.

I learned to speak a language spoken solely behind the White

House gates. I learned the difference between the EOP (the Executive Office of the President) and the WHO (the White House Office). I learned to use the acronyms OPE, IGA, OFL, OVP, PPO, DPC (where I worked), NEC, and OPC in my everyday lingo. I realized that learning politics wasn't different from learning physics or chemistry: it takes lots and lots and lots of time spent feeling confused and hopeless before that lightbulb turns on.

After just five months, I was hired to serve as full-time staff in the office. My job title was Policy Assistant, but I was really the Chief of Staff—basically, I made sure everyone was always doing *their* job. My hours became even longer. I hired and managed six interns per year. I helped with communication between the Director, Jonathan Greenblatt, and the various staff in the office, some of whom were on temporary assignments with our team before returning to their jobs in other agencies or foundations. And I worked closely with the Director to execute the President's social innovation agenda. This included promoting the SIF's successes through blog posts and big events, and facilitating partnerships between the government and the private sector. We also helped manage national service programs like AmeriCorps. One of my favorite parts of the job was helping to decide where the President and First Lady would volunteer every January on the Martin Luther King Jr. Day of Service.

Every day in the White House was different. Some projects developed slowly, over time, waiting for "small wins" like getting a White House blog post published. Similarly, entire weeks could be engulfed by "fire drills"—which is White House speak for "DROP EVERYTHING AND DO THIS!!!!!"

But perhaps most excitingly, after I was hired, I was given my own policy portfolio, which basically meant I had to be an expert within the White House on certain topics. If someone requested a briefing on one of those topics, or a relevant statistic or ideas on what needed changing, I was the person to provide it. At first, a big part of my portfolio was helping to manage a program called Pay for Success. I shared this portfolio with my coworker Annie Donovan, a brilliant woman who has spent her career in community development, working to make sure that low-income communities across America receive economic investments and opportunities.

Pay for Success was, at the time, a brand-new approach to funding government projects. The idea was that instead of paying for a program before results were achieved, the government would partner with a business, which would pay for the project up front. If outside evaluators deemed the project successful, the investing business would make a small profit. If not, the government didn't have to worry about losing money. Sounds basic, but at the time it was totally revolutionary, and it has created more efficient social programs around the country.

One Pay for Success project was launched in Salt Lake County, Utah. It was based on the idea that many low-income kids don't get access to good early education, like pre-K, and as a result, some will require more expensive special education services and ultimately receive fewer economic opportunities as adults. So the county started an experiment to enroll kids in pre-K, hoping to save money and—more importantly—to improve prospects for low-income kids in Utah. And it's working! The project is ongoing and has enrolled several hundred kids in pre-K, improving their education and saving the government hundreds of thousands of dollars.

I loved everything about Pay for Success. It embodied what

had drawn me to government in the first place: the goal of making people's lives better with inventive approaches. Approaches that created tangible results.

I loved my job and not knowing exactly what each week would look like. I embraced the challenge of new policy projects that landed on my desk. But despite being used to surprises, nothing could have prepared me for the day I was given the most important project of my young career.

One afternoon, I was invited to join a meeting with several policy staffers who handle immigration affairs. Our office conference room featured giant photos—called jumbos—taken by Pete Souza, the President's photographer. Staffers usually got to choose which jumbos they hung up near their desks, and they were usually relevant to policies we worked on. Our team chose images of President Obama signing the Serve America Act and volunteering on the Martin Luther King Jr. Day of Service.

The meeting also included professionals from Jewish nonprofits that provide health and social services to Jewish families across America, especially Holocaust survivors. As I looked at the attendees, I wondered what could possibly bring such disparate portfolios together. What did immigration policy staffers have to do with these Jewish organizations?

I quickly learned that these groups weren't as disparate as I had initially thought. A policy staffer shared a fact that stopped me cold: there are more than 120,000 Holocaust survivors living in the United States, and 25 percent of them—if not more—may be living in poverty. Many live alone and can't afford to get assistance with basic things like feeding themselves or using the bathroom. I also learned that many are afraid to sign up for government services because of the trauma of being registered, deported, imprisoned, attacked, and tortured by the German government during the war or the Soviet regime after the war. The side effects of their untreated trauma prevented them from getting the services they needed and deserved so many years later. They lived through some of the worst atrocities committed against humanity, but their suffering had not ended. They were survivors, but now they were dying. It was up to us to help.

I thought of my parents and their trajectory from Morocco to Paris to Florida. My own experiences as a young immigrant were at the core of my identity and my patriotism. I was heartbroken to learn about this group of vulnerable immigrants *from my own community* struggling all over again.

Let me back up a bit. When I was young, I voraciously read books about the Holocaust. Some of them were written by people who were just kids when they were taken from their homes and sent to death camps. Some were historical fiction, stories about people who weren't real but lived through experiences of real people at that time.

I've learned that many of my Jewish friends used to read these books too. We knew the stories of grandparents or more-distant relatives who were victims and survivors. But we wanted to go beyond individual stories. We wanted to understand the *how* and the *what,* because we knew there would never be an answer to *why.*

My favorite book was *I Have Lived a Thousand Years* by Dr. Livia Bitton-Jackson. She was born in 1931 in Czechoslovakia and was just thirteen when she was forced to live in Jewish ghettos before being sent to Auschwitz and other concentration camps. Her beloved father died in the camps, while she, her mother, and her brother survived.

Livia's book ended as a lot of Holocaust memoirs do: she immigrated to the United States. After the Holocaust, many survivors left Europe for places like Israel and the United States, hoping to get distance from the unimaginable pain. And to start a new story. Nothing could change the loss of loved ones, memories, and homes or the physical and emotional trauma so many had endured. But the United States could be a haven where survivors like Livia could start a new life, get married, have children, go to school, and work. Immigration created opportunities and—most of all—allowed for survival.

For me, this was always the end of the story. I found comfort in knowing Livia's book ended this way too—she was safe and surrounded by family. It meant that things could be right again. This idea was shattered as I sat around the conference table at the White House, learning about all the ways survivors continued to suffer in the United States of America, the place that was supposed to be their haven.

I'd known that the world was not as fair as I wanted it to be when I was a kid, of course, but I guess I was still clutching tightly to that triumphant narrative about Holocaust survivors living in America. Even at twenty-three, I wanted to believe that, for survivors, immigrating had led to a happily-ever-after.

In that moment, I felt so naive. I was shaken, and that surprised me. I had been working in policy for over a year, and my job was basically all about how the Obama Administration could alleviate different forms of suffering. I read and wrote and talked about poverty, unemployment, and health care disparities all day long. It was my job to know the statistics, and to serve the public by trying to find a solution. But it was *work,* and always separate from my life beyond the White House gates.

I could barely sit still. I felt a tight knot forming in my chest. Judaism was, and is, deeply important to my personal life. But it was just that—personal. Discussing policy focused on the Jewish community was completely new for me. More than ever, I felt that I had a stake in the discussion.

The Vice President's team was looking for a domestic policy office to spearhead an effort to improve the lives of survivors. I raised my hand to volunteer for the team. I never saw any choice in the matter; I just knew I needed to do something.

Each day at the White House was a reminder of how great our limitations were. For the entire time I worked there, it was a struggle to get funding for the Obama Administration's projects. Funding came from the budget. The budget was approved by Congress. How do you get a divided Congress to support the White House's initiatives?

Every January, we would stay at work until the wee hours of the morning preparing documents for what we called the PB, short for the President's Budget. This is a proposal that the White House sends to Congress annually with the President's recommendations for federal spending. For weeks, I spent most of the night glued to my desk, eating greasy takeout food with my best friend in the office, Dave Wilkinson, only occasionally glancing up from my computer screen. I worked so late on some nights that by the time I left the office, the Metro was closed and I had to wait for a cab in the middle of Washington's frigid winter. As my whole body shuddered inside my parka and I breathed hot air into my scarf to warm my face, I wondered why on earth I had ever moved from Houston to Washington, or left Florida to begin with.

Once the PB process was over, we were usually disappointed. Most of what our office proposed was ignored by Congress. As a result, we would spend the remainder of the year trying to figure out how to advance the President's agenda without federal funding or cooperation from Congress. That meant conducting smart publicity—getting the word out about important matters so that other people could do something about them. It also meant helping President Obama develop Executive Actions—things the President has the power to do without the approval of Congress.

My work on the Holocaust survivor project was no exception to our constant dilemma: How do you start a White House initiative from scratch? Where do you get the funding to even begin?

You start with a young policy assistant, like me.

One thing I always do when I dive into a new project is make lists. A few days after that first meeting on Holocaust survivors' struggles, I filled a ten-page document with questions I didn't have concrete answers to: How many Holocaust survivors live in America? How many are living in poverty? Where do they live? How many live alone? What are the activities they need help with? What are the kinds of government programs they could have access to? How much money would it take to make sure their needs are met?

Then I got to work pulling every lever I could in hopes that something would stick.

I started collaborating with Mark Hanis, a White House Fellow in the Office of the Vice President. We sat through meetings, wrote memos, and looked everywhere for experts. At first, I secretly hoped that people would just tell us what to do. Because the truth is, in policy, you don't always know. It's impossible to be an expert at everything. Usually, you're going to need to call in reinforcements.

To get more information, we held meetings with policy experts, social workers, and heads of nonprofits that care for Holocaust survivors. And to each question I asked I got an answer that was more complicated than I wanted it to be. I learned that we don't know exactly how many survivors there are in the United States; we can only estimate the number as roughly 120,000. I also learned that a lot of survivors were already getting government services, but we didn't know if it was enough to address their needs. This is actually the case for *countless* older people in America, not just Holocaust survivors.

I was consumed with finding a way to change these horrible statistics, but the work was so far over my head. I didn't have a social work degree or expertise on the health and social service needs of the elderly. And although I had spent years building useful skills like writing presidential memos and hosting White House events with dozens of VIPs, those seemed kind of silly next to what I needed now.

Somehow, I had become responsible for coming up with millions of dollars' worth of services for tens of thousands of elderly people scattered across America. I felt powerless, and I felt the weight of knowing this was the most important thing I had ever had to do.

I needed more expertise. I needed reinforcements.

I found Aviva Sufian.

Aviva was in her late thirties and had shiny blond curls that framed her heart-shaped face. She wore wire-rimmed glasses and always smiled with her eyes when she spoke. Like me, she looked a lot younger than she was. I first got to know Aviva after reaching out to staff at the Department of Health and Human Services, hoping that they might be able to collaborate on this project. They instantly mentioned her name, and I soon learned why.

Aviva had spent most of her career serving older Americans and people with disabilities. She had worked, since the very beginning of President Obama's first term, in the Social Security Administration before being named the Director of Regional Operations at the Administration for Community Living at the Department of Health and Human Services. I know—that's an absurdly long title, but it basically meant that her job was to help advance programs and services that improve the lives of older adults and people with disabilities. Prior to that, she had worked for the New York City Department for the Aging as well as a non-profit organization that funded services for Holocaust survivors living in New York City.

In other words, she was *exactly* the person our team needed. She had the experience, the expertise, and the charisma to help pull our initiative together.

I was instantly struck by Aviva. She was dedicated to her work but knew how to be lighthearted and often found a way to make me laugh, even when the work was somber. There was very little she didn't know. Whenever I had a question, she would not only answer it but also show me the questions I should have been asking.

And like me, she really, really cared about this community.

Slowly, the policy portfolio began taking shape. We came up with a four-point plan for how the Administration could help.

1. Expand a service program called AmeriCorps VISTA (Volunteers in Service to America) to create more positions for young people to spend a year providing direct service and companionship to Holocaust survivors. This one was fairly easy to do, because my office worked closely with AmeriCorps VISTA and I knew exactly who to talk to.

2. Encourage outside organizations, such as the Jewish Federations of North America, to help build a private fund that would help pay for health and social services for survivors across America.

3. Propose our own fund, the Survivor Assistance Fund, which would go into the President's Budget.

4. Appoint the first-ever Special Envoy for U.S. Holocaust Survivor Services. This person would reach out to the community, learn more about their needs, and fight for policies that would improve their lives. Aviva was perfect for the job.

As these pieces fell into place, there was just one remaining question: how would we announce this shiny new White House Holocaust Survivor Initiative?

Each White House office speaks a slightly different lingo, but I can guarantee that there is one word that every policy person inside the White House gates is familiar with: *rollout.* A rollout is simply how you announce a policy project, from who delivers the news to which news outlets write about it. If you are announcing something brand-new, like a grant program or a focus on a major social issue, you have to think about how to make the moment as big as possible.

In the White House, you never knew when your rollout moment was coming. You could work for months on a project only to have it get tabled because something else needed your time. Then you could also discover with less than twenty-four hours' notice that President Obama would be making the ideal speech in which to announce your project, and suddenly you're thrown into preparations. (This happened several times during my job at the White House, and though I often complained to myself, I loved the adrenaline rush.)

One day we learned that a major Jewish relief organization called the American Jewish Joint Distribution Committee (JDC) was holding its one hundredth anniversary celebration in Washington, and Vice President Biden was scheduled to speak at the event. It was the perfect opportunity to announce our four-point plan and to show our commitment to the community of Holocaust survivors. Plus, whenever a very famous politician announces your work, you know you've done a good job!

On the day of the event, I was so anxious I could barely eat. All my hard work was about to be shared with the world. I took a taxi to the conference center where the gala was taking place. When I arrived, I looked for familiar faces among the hundreds of people I had never met. The room was filled with the sound of clanging dishes and silverware, and of polite laughter and conversation as people waited for the program to start. I spotted Aviva making conversation with some of her former coworkers from the Jewish community. I stood on the side of the stage, where other staff were waiting, my eyes and fingers glued to my BlackBerry as I tracked emails coming in every few seconds about the Vice President's arrival. It was so strange to think that soon, these strangers in formal wear would be learning about a project that had been so

close to my heart for so many months. I closed my eyes, taking in the last few moments of privacy with this project—*my* project—before it got unveiled to the world.

Before I could even take a breath, I felt the room erupt into powerful applause as guests realized that Vice President Biden had arrived. He walked up onstage and took his place on the podium. I took a seat at a table nearby. As I looked up at Biden and listened to him deliver his remarks, I almost forgot I had written some of the words he was saying and crafted the very policy he was now presenting to the public. I could hear the passion and commitment to service in his voice. He wasn't doing this just for the headline or the photo op—he truly, deeply cared about this community of impoverished Holocaust survivors. For years, many members of the Jewish community had referred to Vice President Biden as an honorary Jew—a humorous title, but one that reflected his commitment to the Jewish community. As I looked around the room, I saw the faces of people who after years of often thankless work with Holocaust survivors were finally hearing their efforts being validated. I heard clapping and even some tears as the Vice President announced the improvements we hoped to make in survivors' lives. And I got to be a part of that.

After the speech, I felt a wave of relief. "This is happening," I thought. "No turning back now." The rollout was just getting started.

Over the next few months, we continued our good work. We delivered on the promises the Vice President made at the JDC event. We partnered with the Corporation for National and Community Service (CNCS) to finalize the plans for the Ameri-Corps VISTA program. We hosted meetings at the White House with heads of organizations like the Association of Jewish Family and Children's Agencies, who were collaborating with us on the public-private partnership fund, which we hoped could lead to $30 million for Holocaust survivor services.

Then there was the budget. In keeping with my annual tradition, I stayed at work far too late throughout January, pulling together the PB, eating greasy food with Dave, and later shivering outside while I waited for my cab, but feeling much more fulfilled than I had in previous years. The product of this effort was a brand-new Holocaust Survivor Assistance Fund, a $5 million program that went into the President's Budget proposal to Congress.

And a few months later, *not* in keeping with the annual tradition, Congress actually approved our proposal. I couldn't believe it.

I am reminded of a quote from Dr. Martin Luther King Jr. that I heard President Obama repeat more than once: "The arc of the moral universe is long, but it bends toward justice." There are a lot of ways to interpret this statement. I've always taken it to mean that although fighting for human rights can feel exhausting and hopeless, things can change with time.

For me, and for so many of my dear friends who worked in the White House, our hearts and our minds are rooted deeply in this idea. President Obama inspired us to accept a call to action to serve our country. The work was grueling, but sometimes, we could actually see justice manifesting around us.

Soon after Aviva started her job as the Special Envoy for U.S. Holocaust Survivor Services, she set out on a listening tour. She visited cities with big communities of Holocaust survivors—places like Miami, Philadelphia, and New York City—where she met directly with survivors and their families, taking careful notes about their needs and working with organizations on how to better leverage resources for their communities.

She invited me to join her on a visit to a group of survivors in Williamsburg, Brooklyn. I immediately accepted her invitation. After devoting more than a year to working on this issue, I hadn't yet had the chance to spend any extended time with a Holocaust survivor, to hear about their struggles in person, and to listen directly to their feedback on the work I was doing.

We took the Amtrak train early that morning from Washington's Union Station to New York's Penn Station. From there, we rode a taxi all the way to Williamsburg, and I instantly felt like I was entering another time.

There are many communities that have contributed their stories to Brooklyn, and one of them is the Orthodox Jewish community. Tens of thousands of very strictly practicing Jews, known as Hasidic Jews, live in Williamsburg, including Holocaust survivors and their descendants. After the war, in the 1940s and 1950s, some survivors settled in Williamsburg, hoping to put an end to their Holocaust stories and start anew. But decades later, many are struggling to get the care they need as they age.

During my visit, Aviva brought me to several meetings. One of those was in a tiny conference room of a Jewish social service agency. The space was only slightly larger than the table inside it, which was worn down and surrounded by mismatched chairs. The walls were bare, save for a few framed pictures of community religious leaders.

As I entered the room, I felt a tight knot in my chest, one I had managed to ignore for months as I dove into the work. But now there was no turning away.

Almost everyone present was a survivor. All were women in their eighties and nineties, and most of them wore wigs—a religious custom for Orthodox married women. Also in keeping with Jewish tradition, they wore long-sleeved shirts and long skirts.

I sat next to Aviva, who confidently found a chair as she shared a brief exchange in Yiddish with a survivor. I had no idea what they were saying, but I smiled as though I did. The survivor noticed me smiling and said something in Yiddish in my direction. I nervously nodded, hoping she couldn't tell that I didn't understand her.

One of the leaders of the organization that provides direct services for the survivors came into the room and closed the door behind her. Everyone took their seats. I pulled out my official White House notebook, a bright green hardcover with the word *RECORD* printed across the front. This wasn't the kind of meeting where I needed to take notes, but it helped to feel like I was doing something. I was certain that at some point, someone would realize that I was only twenty-four and wonder if I even knew what I was doing.

We introduced ourselves, thankfully in English, and the survivors started talking about the struggles their community faces. A lot of their challenges aren't too different from those of other older people: they need help around their home to do daily tasks like bathing and preparing meals as well as outside their home to get to doctor's appointments and participate in community events. Holocaust survivors, like most Americans, want to remain in their homes and communities as they age and need some additional support to do so. Given their experiences during World War II and the trauma they endured, their desire to stay at home runs deep—they are determined to maintain their freedom and independence and to never again be in a place in which they aren't fully in control of their daily lives. And for those who need to move out of their homes and into nursing homes, they need the places to be trauma-informed—to minimize aspects of nursing home life that are potentially retraumatizing, like uniforms and rigid schedules. Giving these survivors this kind of care was at the heart of what we were trying to do.

At first, I was terrified to speak up, feeling the weight of the responsibilities I had taken on. But the energy in the room was so warm and welcoming that I felt comfortable chiming in, telling them about our policy efforts and how our work hoped to alleviate their challenges. I asked them questions about their needs for costly household items, like mattresses—needs I hadn't thought about before. I wanted to learn about everything our work had missed so I could go back to my desk and figure out how to help.

All the while, I heard a voice in my head. A voice of guilt and sadness wondering why I hadn't known about this issue sooner. And fear that I hadn't done enough. Despite these feelings, I let myself get lost in watching Aviva, who was so poised as she led the conversation, toggling between Yiddish and English. She too was young—the second-youngest person in the room—but she spoke with determination and confidence, as if she knew she belonged.

At the end of the meeting, one of the survivors, a tiny woman with kind eyes and deep wrinkles, approached Aviva and me. She had white hair pulled back in a bun, and a youthful, cheery expression. She handed us a giant jigsaw puzzle in a big, beautiful wooden frame. The puzzle had a colorful design with red and blue geometric shapes interspersed with bright yellow Stars of David. Clearly, it had taken hours to put together. At the bottom of the frame was an engraving, thanking Aviva for her service to their community. I choked back tears as Aviva accepted this gift.

On the train ride home to DC, I let those tears out, thinking of that tiny lady and her jigsaw puzzle. I felt undeserving of her generosity. After everything she had been through—and everything she continued to go through—*she* was still somehow giving something to *us*. It was supposed to be the other way around.

I love policy and politics. I treasured the adrenaline rushes and the late nights in the freezing cold (no matter how much I complained!). But on that day—that most memorable day—I remembered what I'd come to the White House for.

Immigration is a rite of passage for children in my family. My ancestors, Spanish Jews, fled their homes for fear of losing their lives in the fifteenth century. My paternal grandmother moved from France to Morocco as a child to escape Nazi persecution. My parents both became childhood immigrants during the sixties, joining a mass exodus of Jews from Morocco to France. And at the age of seven, I made the rite of passage when I emigrated from France to the United States.

Immigration changed the trajectory of my life. It is what makes me an American. I am so proud of my country, and I am inspired by the freedom that so many have sought in coming here. From the day it was founded, the United States has been a safe haven, opening its doors to refugees and immigrants from every continent. It was no different for my family, and I feel indebted to this country for all my successes. It sounds dramatic, but it's true: I have gotten to live my American Dream.

But far too many have not. Working on policies to improve Holocaust survivors' lives, and spending that pivotal afternoon with them in Brooklyn, reminded me of what President Obama had fought for on his way to the presidency and of what his Administration stood for. I am humbled to have been a part of a team of people who gave their all every day to make America a safe haven for everyone, regardless of race, gender, sexuality, country of origin, or age.

Although that meeting is long gone and Brooklyn is hundreds of miles away, I still sometimes feel like I'm in that room. I often think of the survivors in Brooklyn and all around the country. "Never Forget" is a saying I've heard many times in reference to the Holocaust. For me, that saying has become "Always Remember." You know that Martin Luther King Jr. quote I mentioned earlier, the one President Obama likes to use in his speeches? I felt the arc bend slightly that day—and I can't wait to feel that again.

A GIRL'S GUIDE TO GETTING INTO GOVERNMENT

Entering the workforce is scary—we know! So to make your journey easier, we thought we'd offer examples of a few pathways into a public service job. Don't worry if you don't have your whole life mapped out. (Most of us don't!) It's often true that the path you take only makes sense looking back.

That being said, it's helpful to know where to begin. This list doesn't include every way to enter public service, of course, but we hope it helps get you started. And for those of you still in school, at any age, we've got you covered! It's never too early, or too late, to get involved in public service.

The White House Internship Program

Let's begin with the way many of us got our start. In the Obama Administration, a number of staffers (including half of the contributors to this book) began their White House careers as interns. While it's a highly competitive program (depending on the administration, thousands of students may apply for fewer than two hundred spots), it's a great way to get White House experience and position yourself to get hired for open political appointments down the line. As of publication date, the White House internship is unpaid, which can be a financial hardship for many (and unfortunately, unfairly perpetuates socioeconomic inequality in the United States). If you're a student, check with your university about scholarships for students pursuing public service internships.

Hot tip: There's a second White House internship program just for the Office of Science and Technology Policy. If you're interested in the law and/or policy as it relates to science and technology, this is the internship for you!

Just remember . . . your White House internship experience will vary depending on who sits in the Oval Office. While it's not a requirement that your beliefs align with those of the president you work for, whoever is in office will affect your experience and willingness to carry out the responsibilities of the job. Besides, no one wants to work twelve-hour days for a boss they can't stand.

Intern for an Elected Official or Government Office

The White House Internship Program isn't the only internship worth exploring. And depending on who is in the White House, it might not be all that interesting to you. Particularly for students, interning for an elected official or government office (including agencies) is a great way to get public service experience on your résumé and make contacts for your job search down the line. Unfortunately, many internships are unpaid. Check with your school or university to see if you are eligible for scholarships or even school credit for unpaid internships. Bonus: When you work hard in an internship, people often notice and want to hire you after you graduate! Internships can often be found on the web pages of government agencies, but don't be afraid to pick up the phone and ask where you can apply. Usually, government offices have a main line you can call.

Volunteer, Intern, or Work for a Political Campaign

You're never too young to get involved with a political campaign. There are elections nearly every year, and if there's a candidate running in your community who you believe in, reach out to their staff and ask how you can get involved. Whether it's stuffing envelopes, knocking on doors, phone-banking, or just bringing snacks to campaign headquarters, even the youngest volunteers are appreciated.

By the way, a great way to get a job in public service is to work for an elected official before they're elected, as a volunteer, an intern, or a staffer. Candidates who win often need to fill a new office with staff. And many offices see turnover of staff after reelection victories. Putting in good work and long hours on a campaign is an excellent way to land a job in public service. In fact, many people at the Obama White House, especially in the first term, worked on the 2008 campaign. Plus, the bonds you make in the trenches with your fellow campaigners are truly unbreakable.

USAJOBS

On USAJOBS.gov you can apply for positions with federal agencies (like the Department of Justice or Health and Human Services). NASA has even recruited astronauts from this site! And while there are some White House jobs listed, we should note that you won't find White House political appointments (like most of us had) here. For those, you'll want to go through the Presidential Personnel Office (see below).

Did you know that more than two million people work for the U.S. federal government? These jobs aren't just in Washington, DC, either—they're all over the country and even the world. In fact, only 9 percent of federal jobs are located in the Washington, DC, metro area. Most federal agencies have regional offices throughout the country. There are also fifty thousand federal jobs overseas!

Hot tip: If you're applying for a federal government job, make sure your résumé follows the federal government template (searchable online). Doing so will increase the chances of your making it through the process.

Presidential Personnel Office

If you're interested in a "noncareer" appointment (also known as a "political" appointment, meaning your job expires with the president's term in office), check out the Presidential Personnel Office (PPO). The website may vary from administration to administration, but PPO is responsible for filling political appointments in the White House and federal agencies. Sometimes it can seem like a black hole for applications, but you just might get contacted for the role of a lifetime.

State, Local, County, and Tribal Government Jobs

Don't forget that public service encompasses more than just the federal level! There are a tremendous number of elected officials—governors, state senators, state representatives, mayors, county executives, and tribal leaders, just to name a few—across the country who need staff. And if you're interested in a particular subject, check out government agencies. State, local, county, and tribal governments are responsible for implementing education policy, environmental policy, the justice system, and beyond. While many of these offices are "political" (you can serve as long as the elected official serves), there are positions at all levels of government that don't expire when the elected official leaves office.

If you're still in school (no matter your age), see if your local government has any positions reserved for students. Some may have roles like student commissioners or student advisory boards. These are great opportunities to step into public service!

The Peace Corps

Interested in public service and global development? The Peace Corps may be for you. Created by President John F. Kennedy in 1961, the Peace Corps sends volunteers on two-year assignments in more than 140 countries around the world. Peace Corps volunteers help communities with issues like girls' education, food security, health, and more. Former Peace Corps volunteers go on to amazing careers . . . such as serving as members of Congress! Since its inception, nearly a quarter of a million Americans have served. Learn more and how to apply at PeaceCorps.gov. Volunteers must be eighteen or older.

AmeriCorps

Originally created as VISTA (Volunteers in Service to America) by President John F. Kennedy in 1965, and designed to alleviate poverty, this organization was the domestic counterpart to the Peace Corps. Over the years, it has become the AmeriCorps we know today and has expanded to become a national service network made up of three primary programs that each take a different approach to improving lives and fostering civic engagement. AmeriCorps members work on issues across the United States like increasing academic achievement, mentoring youth, fighting poverty, sustaining national parks, preparing for disasters, and more. More than 75,000 people serve as AmeriCorps members each year. Learn more and how to apply at Americorps.gov. AmeriCorps members must be eighteen or older.

National Institutes of Health Postbac Program

Public service isn't just for the policy- and politics-obsessed. We need scientists too! The National Institutes of Health (NIH) runs a postbaccalaureate (postbac) program for recent college grads planning to apply to graduate or professional (medical/dental/pharmacy/nursing/veterinary, e.g.) school. It's an amazing opportunity to spend one or two years performing full-time research at the NIH, alongside some of the leading scientists in the world. Learn more at training.nih.gov/trainees/postbacs.

The United States Digital Service (USDS)

In 2014, President Obama launched the first-ever United States Digital Service. It's kind of like a Silicon Valley start-up within the White House. Staffed by a team of digital and technology experts, many of whom are in government for the first time, USDS is working to bring the federal government's digital services in line with the best of the private sector. USDS works across federal government agencies to help them scale up what works and fix what doesn't. Hailing from the top technology companies in the world, USDSers are helping veterans access information about the benefits available to them, all in one place for the very first time. They're helping high school students make more informed decisions about where to go to college by consolidating clear and accurate data on cost, graduation rates, debt, and postcollege earnings. They're helping refugees resettle in the United States by creating digital tools to expedite outdated systems. If you have a background in design, software engineering, or product management or are just interested in the mission, check out USDS.gov/join.

The Presidential Innovation Fellows (PIFs)

Launched by President Obama in 2012, the extremely competitive PIF program (less than 3 percent of applicants are accepted) offers a prestigious

opportunity to join a highly skilled team leveraging outside-industry expertise to government work. PIFs are some of the top innovators from the private sector, nonprofits, and academia. They join the fellowship for a "tour
of duty," bringing their experience in innovation and problem-solving to
the federal government to address some of the country's biggest challenges.
Learn more at PresidentialInnovationFellows.gov.

18F

Like USDS and the PIF program, 18F was also started by President Obama
(in 2012) and recruits from outside sectors to help make government better. Specifically, 18F, named for the cross streets where its headquarters are
in DC (Eighteenth and F Streets NW), is a digital services agency within
the General Services Administration (GSA) that improves government by
upgrading public-facing services like websites and apps, implementing new
laws or other requirements for agencies to use a new technology, and more.
18F offers you a chance to use your skills in technology, data, and design to
make positive change that affects thousands, if not millions, of people. Not a
bad way to serve the public! Visit 18f.gsa.gov/join to apply.

Teach

Did you know that being a teacher in a public school counts as public service? It's true! Teachers are some of our nation's greatest public servants, and
we need more smart, dedicated individuals in our schools. Organizations
like Teach for America, NYC Teaching Fellowships, and Boston Teaching
Residency are great entrées to a career in education or other public service
opportunities.

The Military

The brave men and women of the United States military have committed to
the highest form of public service. The U.S. military has five branches—the
army, navy, marine corps, air force, and coast guard. And if you're interested
in starting your military career as an undergraduate, check out our nation's
five service academies (one for each branch of the military). There's also the
Reserve Officers' Training Corps (ROTC), available at many nonmilitary

universities, which prepares young people to become officers upon gradu-ation. You must be at least eighteen years old (or seventeen with a parent's consent) to enlist in the U.S. military.

Run for Something!

See an issue in your community you want to address? Run for something! You don't have to start with the presidency (actually, please don't start with the presidency). You can start small. Run for school board. Run for town council or county government. Many offices require you to be eighteen or older, and if you are, why wait? Run anywhere you see an opportunity to work on a problem. Check out our friends at runforsomething.net and find out how you can step up and be the change you wish to see in the world.

Vote

No matter how you choose to get involved with public service—and even if you don't ever serve—make sure you are registered to vote. In some states, you can register at sixteen or seventeen. And in some states, you can vote in the primary election at seventeen if you'll be eighteen for the general election. If you're already registered, make sure your friends and family are registered too. Find out when your registration deadlines and elections are, and make a plan to vote together. We particularly love Vote.gov and WhenWeAllVote.org.

ACKNOWLEDGMENTS

To the leaders who made us believe yes we could: President Barack Obama, Vice President Joe Biden, First Lady Michelle Obama, and Dr. Jill Biden, thank you. You taught us resilience, hard work, and kindness. You challenged us to fight cynicism and gave us hope. We can never fully repay you for the wisdom you have imparted to us and the opportunities you have created for us, so we pledge to try our very best to pay it forward.

Thank you to our rock star of an agent, Wendi Gu, who believed we had a story to tell, and our fearless editor, Annie Kelley, for helping us tell our stories with grace and depth. Thank you to our creative team—Rachael Cole for your tremendous vision and work to make our book so beautiful; Samantha Hahn for your incredible artwork; Carey Wagner and crew for capturing the spirit of sisterhood in a photograph; and Ames Amore and Aleetha Clanton for helping us shine. Thank you to this badass team of ladies for giving us the chance to share our book with the world.

Jenna Brayton

Thank you to Adam Garber for his vision of the White House film festival and for being gracious enough to include me. Thank you to AFI and especially Bob Gazzale for literally everything. Thank you also to Jillian Maryonovich, Hope Hall, Thomas Kelley, and Ashleigh Axios—awesome film-fest partners and helpers who don't come up nearly enough in the story but who are certainly not forgotten. Thank you to all of my bosses, but especially Nick Pancrazio and Jon Bosscher—the ones who started it all. I have learned so much from all of you, and I wouldn't be here without you. And thank you to everyone else who has championed me over the years. There are far too many of you to name here, but please know that I am enormously grateful and have never forgotten what you've done for me. I wrote this in part for all of you—you have assisted me in so many ways, but the most important has been in helping me find my path. My greatest desire is that this book do the same for the next generation. And most importantly, thank you to Mom and Dad for loving and supporting me, always, no matter what.

Eleanor Celeste

Thank you to every person who shared their precision medicine stories with us. Jennifer, Emily, Katrina, Doug, and countless others, your stories fueled us on the good days and the hard days. Thank you to the PMI team: Stephanie Devaney, DJ Patil, Maya Uppaluru, Fae Jencks, Mina Hsiang, Claudia Williams, Matt Might, Chris Vaccaro, and our West Wing advocates, Kristie Canegallo and David Lopez, for believing I could handle big things and then giving them to me. Meredith Drosback, Nita Contreras, and Molly Dillon, you made me laugh, let me whine, and indulged in fro-yotus at all the right moments, so that more than two years at the White House went by in the blink of an eye. My White House service wouldn't have been possible without three women: Tania Simoncelli, who took a chance on me and cheered me all the way to a full-time position; Jo Handelsman, the science division leader who believed in a summer intern; and Cristin Dorgelo, the fearless leader of us all, who hired me and gave me the space to succeed. Thank you, Professors Rudesill, Walker, and Shane, for creating an opportunity for me to be in DC at the exact right moment and for teaching me about the law. I was a more effective advocate in the White House every day because of what I learned from you. Thank you, Jorge Delgado and Matt Tannenbaum, for letting me sleep on your couch for six months when I first moved to DC and for helping me build a life and family there. Thank you, Victoria Wilbur, Jess Powers, and Katie Burrill, for being part of that family and always drinking wine with me after the long days. Julia and Max, thank you for putting up with me bossing you around every day when we were little so I could figure out how to lead. Thank you, CKV—Stefan, Rika, Anna, Max, Julia, Nancy, and Dad—for demonstrating that when it comes to family, more love is always better. Mom and Dad, I was only able to become the person who had this experience and wrote this chapter because of each twist, turn, and total calamity we went through together and because I knew I could always climb higher with you holding me up. And to an enormous group of family and chosen family who have created a reality where I feel capable of anything: you are all the secret ingredient that makes me possible.

Nita Contreras

Thank you first and foremost to my amazing family. Mom and Dad, you guys have been my biggest champions, lifting me up and always finding a way to say yes to my crazy life adventures. To my little brother, Isan, who means the world to me and who first taught me how to love someone else so completely. To my grandfather and my uncle, who made it possible for me to pursue my educational dreams, without which none of this would have been possible. To my grandmother for sharing her creativity and whimsy, which gave me the will to dream. To my abuelita, whose determination and dream for her children and future grandchildren to have a piece of the American Dream is the reason I'm here. To Caitlin Patton, who is like my sister—thank you for always letting me vent my frustration and for celebrating every small victory. A million thanks to Joani Walsh for bringing me to the White House and being such an incredible boss, mentor, and friend. Thank you to Lillian Salerno, my first DC friend and mentor, who helped give me my first professional win, pushed me into the spotlight, and helped me navigate my career. Thank you to the countless women (and men) who have cheered me on—Melinda, Elle, Molly, and Ashley get a special shout-out. Your friendship and the amazing community I've found in DC have been instrumental to my good fortune.

Molly Dillon

Thank you to the two women who believed in me enough to hire me at the White House in the first place: Racquel Russell and Diana Zarzuelo. My story would not exist without my former boss and forever mentor, Roy L. Austin Jr., always pushing for what is right. ("It's not a heavy lift.") You set quite the bar for all future bosses. Forever indebted to the entire UJO team Roy created . . . I love you guys. Extra thank-yous to my White House big brother and sisters (Luke Tate, Natalia Merluzzi, Becky Monroe, and Peach Soltis) and the foster care crew (JooYeun Chang, Sherry Lachman, Rafael López, Sonali Patel, and Megan Smith): you are some of our nation's finest public servants—it's an honor to know you. Thank you to Sixto Cancel and Jodi Gillette for helping me share this story with care. Raffi Freedman-Gurspan, thank you for your wisdom, words, and friendship. So much gratitude for my 504 sisters, sounding boards, and sanity keepers, Rebecca Fishbein and Christina Padilla. Love to my Hopkins crew—thank you for wrapping your arms around me and my affinity for matching outfits. Thank you to the coolest couple: Val Galasso, for being there every step of the way, and Nick Merrill, for your early read of the proposal . . . and for telling me this wasn't a crazy idea. To my friends of over twenty-five years, Melissa Feinstein and Elisa Redish, so glad I found you at Beth El Preschool. Endless love for my coauthors and the fierce sisterhood you have provided me individually and collectively through the years. None of this would be possible without family. Thank you, Mom, Dad, Josh, and Bubbie (BOTUS). Shout-out to the Highland Park High School Congressional Debate Team. Being a debate nerd can get you to the White House . . . and what's cooler than that? Keep at it.

Kalisha Dessources Figures

Thank you, President Obama and Mrs. Obama, for redefining what was possible for young people like me. For a Black girl of immigrant heritage growing up in suburban New York, you—your story, your success—forever changed my life and its trajectory. You showed me that a brown-skinned girl can belong in the White House. Jordan Brooks: my forever partner in crime. You trusted me, you invested in me, you made an insane amount of room for me to lead. I admire you as a colleague and a friend. Tina Tchen and Valerie

Jarrett, thank you for taking a chance on me. Thanks for looking my twenty-five-year-old self square in the eye and somehow seeing the potential I had to lead this work. I learned the world from you two. Heather Foster and Ashley Allison, you in so many ways gave me the skills I needed to succeed at my post-intern jobs at the White House. Thanks for holding such a high bar for me. And to all the phenomenal women who graced the halls of the White House with me—including those I had the honor to write this with—the lessons I learned watching you all in action are invaluable. To Shomari—the man I'm lucky enough to spend my life with—I confess that the chapter in this book is my second-favorite White House story. My favorite will always be meeting and falling in love with you. And to my family, the crew that fostered my passionate, sometimes-defiant, ambitious, strong-willed, "tough cookie" spirit from day one: Mom and Dad, thank you for always letting me chase my dreams, whatever they were. Kimmy, Shanice, and Leslie-Anne, you girls are the best sisters a girl could have asked for. I'm so proud of each of you. To my best friends, who are family; my many taties; my many cousins; my goddaughter, Vaniyah. To the legacy of love, hard work, and grit that is and always will be Mamie Lunie. And finally, to Grandma Charlotte, my newest angel. I miss you every single day. This one's for you, Nenen. I am because of you.

Andrea R. Flores

Thank you to Felicia Escobar, Esther Olavarria, and Tyler Moran, for showing me the way to be a public servant. Thank you to Susan Marine, PhD, who believed I could be a leader before I did. Thank you to Stephanie Valencia and Oscar Ramirez, for opening doors and creating new pathways for the Latinx community. Thank you to my family, who collectively raised me to be resilient in the face of disappointment. And a special thank-you to the immigrant rights community, who continue to fight for the human rights of immigrants in a country that too often struggles to deliver them.

Vivian P. Graubard

I thank my lucky stars every day for the many people who have championed me, professionally and personally, throughout my life. My first bosses:

Martin Cuellar, Michael Hornsby, and Jason Smith—thank you for taking a chance on twenty-year-old Viv! My greatest advocates, Todd Park and Mikey Dickerson—thank you for always providing me opportunities to grow, challenge myself, and level up. To the women who graced the White House with their brilliance and helped me navigate its many wonderful challenges: Dawn Mielke, Lynn Overmann, Jai Retter, my brilliant coauthors, and so many others—your friendship, long walks through the White House, and frozen yogurt at the mess made the hard days a little brighter and a lot sweeter. To the many senior advisors of President Obama who have offered me guidance and advice—you'll never know how much your generosity of spirit and time has meant to me. A special thanks to Cecilia Muñoz, my fellow Latina, mentor, and dear friend. To my future husband, Ron: my best friend, my forever focal point, the solid foundation on which I can be free to be myself and pursue all my big, idealistic, sometimes crazy ideas. And finally, a mi familia, Mami, Papi, Hans, and Christian: I would be lost without you. Thank you for your ample patience, your unwavering love, and your endless support. The words do not exist to express how much I love you. Everything I have done is for you. Los amo a todos.

Noemie C. Levy

Thank you to two unstoppable women, Aviva Sufian and Shelley Rood, for your advocacy and grit. Thank you to everyone who worked on the Holocaust Survivor Initiative and to all who are fighting for victims of genocide. Thank you to Jonathan Greenblatt for taking a chance on me and for fearlessly leading the SICP team. Annie Donovan, I can never repay your generosity—you were there through some of my hardest moments and you taught me to fight for those without a voice. To the inimitable Dave Wilkinson, thank you for your enormous heart and for teaching me to hustle for the American people. To my dear friend Rafael López: this country is a better place for families because of you. Endless love and gratitude to the inspiring women who set an example I strive to live up to: Cristin Dorgelo, Jennifer Erickson, Caitlin Fleming, Anna Fogel, Cecilia Muñoz, Helen Pajcic, Sonal Shah, Marta Urquilla. Thank you to the SICP family, especially the brilliant interns. Thank you to Tom Kalil for inviting me into the OSTP family.

Thank you to Robbie Barbero and Kumar Garg for always leaving a chair in your office for me. Thank you to my coauthors for the sisterhood and inspiration. To my sweet friends Emma, Meghan, Molly, Page, Rachel, Raquel, Sigrid, and the Wonderland crew: I thank the fates for having you in my life. To Janet, Marty, Benny, and Gabriela: you have filled my life with the brightest love. Thank you, Max, for the endless giggles, you mystery man. Thank you forever to my parents, Edith and Emmanuel, for sacrificing everything for our American Dream—you made it happen. Finally, thank you, Graham: my greatest fortune was meeting you. I love you.

Taylor Lustig

Thank you, President Obama, for inspiring me to consider public service. Thank you to the Obama family I met along the way for creating and sustaining hope for what we can achieve together with a sense of common purpose, and for never giving up on Yes We Can. To my Obama family colleagues, including my coauthors and our fearless leader, Molly Dillon, you continue to inspire me. Thank you for your friendship. To the women who took a chance on my younger self: Kelly Jin and Natalie Pojman, thank you for believing in me. Kelly, thank you for your mentorship and for the chance to even attempt to fill your shoes for the few weeks you were in Antarctica. Katie Wright, thank you for your genuine mentorship during my first foray in Washington and for helping me navigate the DC professional world. Thank you for encouraging me to apply for the White House internship. Melissa Rogers, thank you for providing the opportunity to work for you in OFBNP and learn from your brilliance and steadfast courage.

Most importantly, thank you to my family. Thank you, Unks, Avi Poster, for encouraging all of us to chase down those hero stories and teaching me what it means to be an activist, a believer, and a change maker. A big heartfelt hug to Lauren Cowen, aka "Al," for your writing and editing guidance throughout this process. Straight-up. Thank you to my sisters, Carli and Madison, for being the best friends and teachers. Thank you for always listening to me but also for telling me when it's time to shut up. Don't forget about me in Chicago #middlechild. Thank you, Mom and Dad, for the opportunity and real encouragement throughout my life to chase any dream. And thank you, Sean, my best friend and support on the front lines. I love you.

Jaimie Woo

Thank you, Vice President Joe Biden, and the whole OVP team. Thank you to Don Graves for valuing my younger self and hiring me. Eternally grateful to Lacy Kline for her endless mentorship; without her, I would not have had this story to tell. Much gratitude to Faisal Amin, Carri Twigg, and Lauren Peterson, whose kindness and encouragement gave me confidence and hope. Lots of love to my work mom and confidante, Kris Rose—I couldn't ask for a better office mate and friend. Thank you to Caira Woods, Cailin Crockett, and Carrie Bettinger-Lopez, women at the White House who gave me community and taught me humility and the value of hard work. Thank you, Ben Harris, Greg Schultz, Michael Schrum, Naseam Alavi, Jamie Lyons, Alex Mackler, Vinay Reddy, and Nate Rawlings for chipping away at my imposter syndrome and always making me feel a part of the family—you have no idea the difference you made. Huge thank-you to the VP's milaides for their patience and help in delivering the VP's Daily Briefing Book. Thank you to Congressman Lloyd Doggett for giving me room to grow in my writing.

Thank you to my fellow female authors and fierce feminists. You inspire me. A million thank-yous to Molly Dillon for asking me to share my story; to Vivian Graubard for her inspiration and faith; to Lexi Kellison, Gabby Arredondo, and Kim Williams for years of support, patience, and friendship; and to Emma Boorboor for her unconditional and true sisterhood. Most importantly, thank you, Mom and Dad, for your love and lessons. Your stories are as important as ever, and I am humbled to be a part of them.

ABOUT YARA SHAHIDI

Yara Shahidi is an actress, model, activist, and breakout star of ABC's Emmy- and Golden Globe–nominated comedy series *black-ish*. She stars as popular teen Zoey Johnson, an ambitious, technologically infatuated high school student. Shahidi currently stars on the *black-ish* spin-off *grown-ish* on Freeform, which explores Zoey's transition to adulthood as well as issues facing both students and administrators in the world of higher education.

Since *black-ish* launched in 2014, Shahidi has been awarded an NAACP Image Award for Outstanding Supporting Actress and a Gracie Award for Female in a Breakthrough Role. She was recently named to *Time* magazine's annual 30 Most Influential Teens list and *Forbes*'s 30 Under 30 list for her television contributions and humanitarianism. Politically engaged and purpose driven, Shahidi launched the platform Eighteen x '18 to empower first-time voters.

In June 2017, Shahidi graduated with honors from the Dwight School in New York City. She attends Harvard University, where she double majors in sociology and African American studies.

ABOUT THE AUTHORS

Jenna Brayton began serving in the White House at age twenty-five and left two weeks before her twenty-seventh birthday. She was a member of the first White House digital team—known as the Office of Digital Strategy (ODS)—which was tasked with helping President Obama find his voice online. She served as Associate Director of Content and Operations, working to help manage content partnerships, communications campaigns, and digital outreach. After leaving ODS, Jenna continued to do advance work for President Obama through the end of his Administration. Originally from Chicago, Jenna currently teaches college courses on politics, policy, public service, and technology.

Eleanor Celeste served in the White House from age twenty-six to age twenty-eight (until the end of the Obama Administration and through the transition), most recently as Assistant Director for Biomedical and Forensic Sciences in the Office of Science and Technology Policy. In that role, she focused on the life sciences, precision medicine, biosafety and biosecurity, privacy and security of health information, patient access to data, emerging biotechnology, and forensic science. She previously served as an intern and as a Policy Advisor in that same office. Originally from Ohio, she holds a bachelor's degree in biology and feminist, gender, and sexuality studies from Wesleyan University, and has a graduate certificate in bio-hazardous threat agents and emerging infectious disease from George-town University. She received a law degree from the Ohio State University. Eleanor currently serves as Associate Director for Research and Develop-ment Communications at Vertex Pharmaceuticals, a biotechnology com-pany in Boston.

Nita Contreras served in the White House from age twenty-five to age twenty-seven (until the end of the Obama Administration) as Assistant Staff Secretary in the Office of the Staff Secretary, where her work focused on compiling the President's Daily Briefing Book. Before joining the White House staff, she served as a political appointee in several areas, ranging from rural development to food safety at the U.S. Department of Agri-culture. Originally from Santa Monica, California, Nita holds a bachelor's degree in international relations from Connecticut College and is complet-ing a master's in energy policy and climate from Johns Hopkins University while working as the Executive Assistant to the Executive Vice President, Corporate Development, and General Counsel of Enviva, a global renewable energy company specializing in sustainable wood biomass.

Molly Dillon served in the White House from age twenty-three to age twenty-seven (until the end of the Obama Administration), most recently as a Policy Advisor for Urban Affairs, Justice and Opportunity in the Domes-tic Policy Council. In that role, she focused on civil rights policy, includ-ing criminal justice reform, LGBTQ rights, women's equality, voting rights, human services, housing, labor, economic mobility, and urban communi-ties. She previously served as an intern and a Policy Assistant in the same office. Originally from Highland Park, Illinois, she graduated Phi Beta Kappa with a bachelor's degree in sociology from Johns Hopkins University and holds a master's in public policy from the Georgetown University McCourt School of Public Policy. After the Administration, Molly served as a Senior Policy Advisor in the Office of the New York Governor. She is currently the

Community Curator and Manager of Programming for an international philanthropic foundation.

Kalisha Dessources Figures served in the White House from age twenty-four to age twenty-six (until the end of the Obama Administration), most recently as a Policy Advisor to the White House Council on Women and Girls, where she led the portfolio on advancing equity for women and girls of color. Her work focused on a range of issues, including exclusionary school discipline policies, juvenile justice reform, STEM education, and economic security. Kalisha previously served in the White House as Staff Assistant for Intergovernmental Affairs and as an intern in the Office of Public Engagement. Before joining the White House staff, Kalisha was a middle and high school math and science teacher in Philadelphia. Originally from New York, she holds a bachelor's degree in labor relations from Cornell University and a master's of science in education from the University of Pennsylvania. Kalisha is currently a PhD student in sociology at Yale University, and continues to do consulting work focused on racial and gender equity.

Andrea R. Flores served in the White House from age twenty-four to age twenty-five as a Policy Assistant on both the Immigration and Rural Affairs teams in the Domestic Policy Council. Her work centered on advocating for commonsense immigration reform and strengthening rural communities. Before joining the White House, Andrea was a presidential appointee at U.S. Citizenship and Immigration Services before returning to the Department of Homeland Security to continue her work on immigration policy in the Secretary's Office. Following her time in the Obama Administration, Andrea was a Regional Policy Director on the Hillary for America campaign. Originally from Las Cruces, New Mexico, Andrea holds a bachelor's degree from Harvard College, where she was elected the first Latinx student body president, and a law degree from Columbia Law School. Andrea is currently an attorney practicing in Washington, DC.

Vivian P. Graubard served in the White House from age twenty-one to age twenty-seven, most recently as a Senior Advisor and Cofounder of the United

States Digital Service, where she led efforts to improve government digital services, including streamlining the immigration process and reducing data loopholes in the gun background-check system. Previously, she served in the White House Office of Science and Technology Policy as a Confidential Assistant and Advisor, focused on combating human trafficking and ending sexual assault on college campuses. She is a proud Latina with Colombian, Cuban, and Puerto Rican roots and was named to the *Time* 30 Under 30 and *Forbes* 30 Under 30 in Law and Policy lists. She holds a bachelor's degree in business administration with a double major in international business and IT from American University. Vivian currently serves as the Director of Strategy for Public Interest Technology at New America.

Noemie C. Levy served in the White House from age twenty-two to age twenty-seven, most recently as a Senior Policy Advisor for partnerships in the Office of Science and Technology Policy, where she helped develop public-private partnerships to advance Obama Administration initiatives. Prior to that role, she served as a Policy Assistant for the Office of Social Innovation and Civic Participation in the Domestic Policy Council. Noemie was born in Paris, France, and immigrated to the United States when she was six years old. She holds a bachelor's degree from Rice University and is currently a medical student at Stanford University.

Taylor Lustig served in the White House from age twenty-two to age twenty-six, most recently as a Policy Advisor for the White House Office of Faith-Based and Neighborhood Partnerships, part of the Domestic Policy Council. Her work focused on community engagement and domestic and international policy issues of concern to the faith community (i.e., everything . . .), interfaith dialogue, and church-state policy. She previously served as a Policy Assistant in the same office. After the White House, Taylor moved over to the Department of Labor, where she served as a political appointee in the Secretary's Office of Public Engagement until the end of the Obama Administration. Originally from Deerfield, Illinois, she holds a dual bachelor's degree in political science and psychology from the University of Texas at Austin (hook 'em!). Taylor is currently a Manager of Government and External Affairs at PepsiCo.

Jaimie Woo served in the White House from age twenty-four to age twenty-five (until the end of the Obama Administration) as a Policy Analyst in the Office of the Vice President. She initially focused on Vice President Biden's Cancer Moonshot initiative, health, and LGBTQ policy, though she later joined his Violence Against Women team and worked on policy and public engagement efforts to combat domestic violence and sexual assault and to improve bystander intervention. Before joining the White House, Jaimie managed economic justice advocacy campaigns for the U.S. Public Interest Research Group. Following her role at the White House, Jaimie served as Congressman Lloyd Doggett's Communications Director in the U.S. House of Representatives, where she was the only female Asian American Pacific Islander (AAPI) to hold said title in all congressional offices throughout her tenure. Jaimie is a Texan, a Floridian, and a proud daughter of Chinese immigrants. She holds a bachelor's degree in cultural anthropology from Duke University and is pursuing a master's degree in communications management at the University of Southern California's Annenberg School of Communications and Journalism.